A Survival Guide to

CRITICAL PATH ANALYSIS

and the Activity on Node Method

To my parents

A Survival Guide to

CRITICAL PATH ANALYSIS

and the Activity on Node Method

Andrew Harrison

Butterworth-Heinemann
Linacre House, Jordan Hill, Oxford OX2 8DP
A division of Reed Educational and Professional Publishing Ltd

A member of the Reed Elsevier plc group

OXFORD   BOSTON   JOHANNESBURG
MELBOURNE   NEW DELHI   SINGAPORE

First published 1997

British Library Cataloguing in Publication Data
Harrison, Andrew
  A survival guide to critical path analysis
  1.   Critical path analysis
  I.   Title
  658.4'032

ISBN 0 7506 3701 3

Typeset by Jane Bigos
Printed and bound by Biddles Ltd, Guildford and Kings Lynn

Contents

Contents

Figures

Tables

Foreword

During my thirty years' experience as a professional engineer, I have always been aware that to be a successful manager, technical skills and experience must be supplemented with a high degree of effectiveness in the planning and control of activities.

Critical path analysis is probably one of the most practical and effective ways of developing these management skills.

As a senior lecturer of business studies and production management, I consider that this book proceeds in a logical manner, and enables the reader to select the appropriate stage relevant to their present knowledge of the technique.

Andrew Harrison has produced what I would call essential reading for those who see a need to improve their planning and control activities. It is recommended without reservation.

Arthur Walton
Warwickshire College, Royal Leamington Spa & Moreton Morrell

Acknowledgement

I would like to express my appreciation to Arthur Walton, former Senior Assistant Director in charge of Management Studies at Warwickshire College, Royal Leamington Spa & Moreton Morrell, for his guidance during the writing of this book.

1 An introduction to critical path analysis

1.1 Introduction

If a project requires various activities (sometimes referred to as tasks) to be carried out towards its completion it would be of benefit to use some sort of system to plan and control the work involved. It is an all too common occurrence that a project will finish late, perhaps due to

- Over-estimating the resources of the organization.
- Under-estimating the time required to finish a particular activity.
- Insufficient information concerning the progress of the project.
- Failing to identify the importance of the prior completion of a preceding activity upon which several succeeding activities depend.
- General deficiencies in planning and control.

By planning the work schedule in advance, management can

- Set realistic target dates.
- Allocate realistic resource levels.
- Control the progress of individual activities, groups of activities and the project as a whole.
- Apply corrective action before any such problems arise which could endanger the project.
- Identify the requirements and the consequences relating to the activities within the project. For example, activity *Build gearbox* is expected to take 4 minutes to complete. What will the effect be on the whole project if the activity actually takes 6 minutes to complete?

1.2 Critical path analysis – a brief overview

Critical path analysis (CPA) is an aid which promotes logical thinking and is often referred to as the Activity on Arrow (AoA) method of network analysis. The effectiveness of CPA is maximized when it is used to analyse projects. In CPA the project is divided into named activities (e.g. *Lay carpets*, *Fit doors* etc.). Every activity must have a definable beginning and a definable end, otherwise CPA becomes ineffective. Each activity is shown pictorially as an arrow, and the relationship (often described as a dependency) between these activities is defined by their relative position to each other. These arrows make-up a network which represents the project. This is known as an Activity on Arrow (AoA) network (sometimes referred to as an arrow diagramming method network or ADM network).

Activities which progress in linked sequence are shown as arrows that follow each other through the network. Figure 1 shows three activities in series.

Figure 1   An example of a series of activities

Activities which occur at the same time, but along different paths (sometimes referred to as chains), are shown as arrows in parallel and are called parallel activities. An example of two paths of parallel activities, with each path containing three activities, is shown in Figure 2.

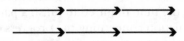

Figure 2   An example of parallel activities

It is also a common occurrence that a network will consist of linked series and parallel activities, as shown in Figure 3.

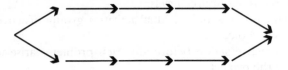

Figure 3   An example network of linked series and parallel activities

The relationship between the different activities is identified by the direction and connection of the arrows. The duration time required to complete each activity is assigned and through the observance of established rules and procedures the network can be drawn. Calculations are made involving the duration times and, as a result, the critical path can be identified.

---

1   Every **activity** must have a definable beginning and a definable end.
2   Each activity (sometimes referred to as a **task**) within a **project** is defined by an **activity arrow**. These activity arrows build up into a **network** which defines the relationship between the activities of a **project**.

---

3   Calculation of the **critical path** establishes the minimum time that is required to complete the overall project. This minimum time is referred to as the **total project time (TPT)**.

4   An **Activity on Arrow (AoA)** network is sometimes referred to as an arrow diagramming method (ADM) network.

1.3   The uses for critical path analysis

CPA was devised in 1957 by the Reamington-Rand Division of the Sperry Rand Corporation for work being carried out for Du Pont concerning scheduling and controlling maintenance shut-downs of large chemical process plants. In 1958 the United States Navy Special Projects Unit used a form of AoA, known as PERT (Program and Evaluation Review Technique), to control the Polaris ballistic missile development programme (the project was completed 2 years ahead of plan). CPA can be used on both small and large projects, in areas such as

- Public sector services (e.g. the reorganization/relocation of a department, or an entire service).
- Commerce (e.g. the reorganization of the services of a banking institution after merging with another).
- Industry (e.g. the one-off project of constructing a dam, motorway or building).
- Maintenance, inspection, repair and shut-down programmes.

1.4   The advantages of critical path analysis

The advantages of CPA include:

- It can be used on a complete project or just a particular section of a project.
- Alternative methods of how an activity could be carried out (e.g. *Fit gearbox to engine*) can be examined both initially and while the project is underway so as to see if the duration time and resources required for the activity can be reduced.
- It provides an accurate record of information concerning a project.
- Management and supervisors can communicate more effectively with their own team, as well as other departments, because everybody will be using the same information.
- Ambiguity encountered through the verbal exchange of information can be greatly reduced.
- It benefits the organization internally through implementation of improved procedures and methods.

- Can influence how the external environment views the posture of the organisation.
- Can be used effectively during value analysis (VA) of a procedure or product which the project represents.
- Management and supervisors can gauge actual progress against planned progress.

CPA can be effective in many areas which may not necessarily be recognized at first as being suitable to its application. CPA could well be of great assistance in:

- Decision making (e.g. starting a new business).
- Ordering systems (e.g. where sub-contractors are used as suppliers).
- Undertaking an assignment or preparing for a practical examination.
- Problem solving (e.g. dealing with a customer complaint).

2 The key elements in an Activity on Arrow network

2.1 An activity

An activity is a task (e.g. *Fit gearbox*) which is performed as a part of the overall project. It is important to remember that the term activity means the passage of time (e.g. *Wait for glue to set*) and does not necessarily mean that actual work (e.g. *Build-up gear train* or *Fit door frame*) is carried out. Each activity is pictorially defined as an individual arrow (often referred to as an activity arrow). Therefore, the activities *Fit gearbox* and *Fit clutch* will be shown as two separate arrows and, as a result, each arrow will have a unique identity, as shown in Figure 4.

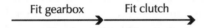

Figure 4 The unique identity of two activities

The tail of an arrow represents the start of the activity. The head of the arrow represents the finish of the activity. A preceding activity occurs before a succeeding activity. A succeeding activity is sometimes referred to as a following activity. Activities which take place one after the other along the same path are known as a series of activities, as shown in Figure 5. An activity in series is nominally dependent upon the prior completion of its predecessor (i.e. the succeeding activity cannot start until the preceding activity has been completed). This form of relationship between a preceding activity and a succeeding activity can normally be referred to as a finish to start (FS) relationship.

Figure 5 A series of activities

Activities which take place along different paths are known as parallel activities. The two paths shown in Figure 6 can take place at the same time. A path of activities can also be referred to as a chain of activities.

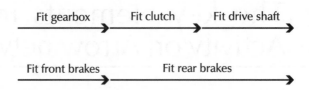

Figure 6 An example of parallel activities

---

1 The **tail** of an arrow represents the start of an activity.
2 The **head** of an arrow represents the finish of an activity.
3 A **preceding activity** occurs prior to a **succeeding activity**. A succeeding activity occurs after a preceding activity. For example, if activity *Move filing cabinets* precedes activity *Move computers*, the activity *Move filing cabinets* occurs before activity *Move computers*.

The actual description of an activity (e.g. *Fit exhaust*) is often defined only as a letter which is shown above the shaft of the arrow (the letter I is not used because it can be confused with number 1 when a network is drawn free-hand). The estimated duration time, which will be required to complete the activity, is shown underneath the shaft. In Figure 7 the activity:

- *Fit gearbox* is defined as the letter J and has a duration time of 5 minutes.
- *Fit clutch* is defined as the letter K and has a duration time of 3 minutes.
- *Fit drive shaft* is defined as the letter L and has a duration time of 2 minutes.
- *Fit front brakes* is defined as the letter S and has a duration time of 7 minutes.
- *Fit rear brakes* is defined as the letter T and has a duration time of 8 minutes.

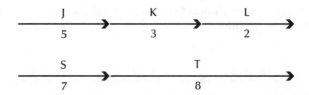

Figure 7 Assigning the unique identity and duration time of an activity

It should be noted that the actual length of the arrow does not define the duration time that the activity takes to complete. For example, an activity which takes 5 minutes to complete will not be identified by an arrow which is longer than the arrow of an activity which only takes 3 minutes. The preceding activity is drawn to the left of the succeeding activity so that the network is drawn from left to right as time progresses.

The extract from a network of activities shown in Figure 8 shows the description of each activity and its duration time. The activities *Fit exhaust, Fit mirrors, Fit front lights, Fit wheels* and *Fit rear lights* must be completed before the activity *Test lights* can be started.

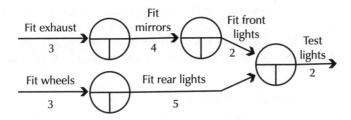

Figure 8   Extract from an Activity on Arrow (AoA) network

1	The preceding activity is drawn to the left of the succeeding activity so that the network is drawn from left to right as time progresses.

2.2   The time elements of an activity

The time elements of an activity can be studied through the following scenario:

> The time frame available to complete activity *Paint car doors* is between 9.00 a.m. and 10.00 a.m. It is estimated that activity *Paint car doors* will have a duration time of 45 minutes. The succeeding activity is planned to start at 10.00 a.m.

2.2.1   Earliest starting time (EST)

This is the earliest time within the time frame at which the activity can start. The EST for the activity will be 9.00 a.m. If the activity was to start before 9.00 a.m. it could start before a preceding activity had finished and could thus affect the logic of the network and the total project time (TPT).

2.2.2   Duration time

This is the amount of time required to complete the activity. The form by which the duration time is defined (e.g. minutes; days etc.) may not always appear in the column heading of the table of activities for the project (Table 1).

2.2.3   Earliest finishing time (EFT)

This is the earliest time within the time frame by which the activity can finish without affecting the total project time (TPT) or the logic of the network. The EFT for the activity will be 9.45 a.m. because the earliest starting time (EST) is 9.00 a.m. and the duration time is 45 minutes.

2.2.4   Latest starting time (LST)

This is the latest time within the time frame at which the activity can start without possibly affecting the total project time (TPT) or the logic of the network. The LST for the activity will be 9.15 a.m. If the activity was to start later, the activity would not be finished by 10.00 a.m. thus affecting the succeeding activity.

2.2.5   Latest finishing time (LFT)

This is the latest time within the time frame by which the activity can finish without affecting the total project time (TPT) or the logic of the network. The LFT for the activity will be 10.00 a.m. thus requiring a LST of 9.15 a.m.

2.2.6   Total project time (TPT)

This is the minimum amount of time required to complete a project. The TPT is the sum of the combined total of the duration times of the activities within the project which occur along the critical path of the network. An activity which has not started by its latest starting time (LST), or has not finished by its latest finishing time (LFT) could affect the TPT (i.e. the project could finish late).

2.3   The table of activities

The activities which make-up a project can be tabulated in a variety of ways (often referred to as a table of activities). Three different examples of the tabling of the activities of the same project are shown as Table 1, Table 2 and Table 3.

Table 1   Example 1 of a table of activities

Activity	Preceding activity	Duration*
A	–	3
B	A	9
C	A	7
D	A	4
E	B, C	5
F	D	3
G	E	4
H	E	6
J	F, G, H	4
K	J	3

* Duration time in days.

Table 1 shows how each of the activities of the project is defined by a unique letter which results in each activity having a unique identity. The first column, headed Activity, denotes the immediate activity under consideration. The second column, headed Preceding activity, denotes the activity (or activities) which occur before the activity under the first column (e.g. the preceding activities B and C occur before the succeeding activity E). The third column denotes the duration time required to complete the activity in the first column.

Table 2   Example 2 of a table of activities

	Activity	Precedes activity	Duration (days)
Opening	(A	B, C, D	3
	B	E	9
	C	E	7
	D	F	4
	E	G, H	5
	F	J	3
	G	J	4
	H	J	6
	J	K	4
Closing	(K	–	3

In Table 2, the first column denotes which activities occur at the Opening of the network (i.e. activity A), and which activities occur at the Closing of the network (i.e. activity K). The opening and closing of the network is also identified by the use of an open bracket next to the relevant activity.

In Table 2 the column headed Precedes activity contains the succeeding activity, or activities, which will occur after the preceding activity detailed in the column headed Activity. For example, succeeding activities G and H occur after preceding activity E.

A simple scenario for the manufacture of a gearbox

Another way of describing the activities which make up a project is by a scenario case study with an accompanying list of activities and duration times. For example:

All raw materials and castings are distributed to the machine shop, upon which the rough machining of the gears, the shafts and the gearbox castings can separately take place. The gears and shafts are separately hardened and stress-relieved after rough machining and before grinding. After rough machining, the gearbox castings are finished machined. All machined components are then collectively inspected prior to assembly of the gearbox components.

The scenario is analysed so that the various processes undertaken in the project are divided into timed activities which are listed in a table, as shown in Table 3.

Table 3 Example 3 of a table of activities

ID	Activity	Duration
A	Distribute raw materials and castings to machine shop	3d
B	Rough machine gears from raw materials	9d
C	Rough machine shafts from raw materials	7d
D	Rough machine gearbox castings	4d
E	Harden and stress-relieve gears and shafts	5d
F	Finish machine gearbox castings	3d
G	Grind gears	4d
H	Grind shafts	6d
J	Inspect finished machined components	4d
K	Assemble gearbox components	3d

In Table 3, the column headed ID denotes, by the use of a unique identity letter, each of the activities shown in the column headed Activity. The column headed Duration, denotes the duration time of the appropriate activity (e.g. *Grind Shafts* 6 days).

1 An activity which precedes the succeeding activity occurs before the succeeding activity.
2 An activity which succeeds the preceding activity occurs after the preceding activity.
3 No succeeding activity can start until its preceding activities have been completed.

2.4 An event

An event has no duration time, nor does it take up any resources, and defines the position between the finish of a preceding activity and the start of a succeeding activity. An event is depicted as a circle, as shown in Figure 9, and is often referred to as a node. An event which represents the start of an activity is called a tail event. An event which represents the finish of an activity is called a head event. The head event of an activity will have a higher unique event number than the tail event of the activity. The event which represents the start of the network is referred to as the start event of the network (sometimes referred to as the opening event, the beginning event or the beginning node of the network). The event which represents the finish of the network is referred to as the finish event of the network (sometimes referred to as the closing event, the closing node or the end event of the network).

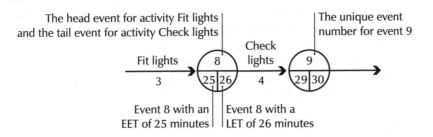

Figure 9 An event

An event is segmented into one top half-segment and two quarter-segments at the bottom. These segments can be explained as follows:

• The top half-segment contains the unique event number which is assigned to each event as the drawing of the network progresses. The start event of the network is identified and referred to as event 1 or node 1. Each succeeding event is identified with a higher number than the last preceding event (this process is referred to as sequential numbering) as the network progresses from left to right.

- The bottom left-hand quarter segment contains the earliest event time (EET) for that particular event which is the earliest time by which that event can take place. The EET occurs at the same time as the:
  — Earliest starting time (EST) of an activity, which is the earliest time by which an activity can start without affecting the total project time (TPT) or the logic of the network.
  The EET also occurs at the same time as the:
  — Earliest finishing time (EFT) of an activity when there is only one activity finishing at the event or if an activity finishing at the event forms part of the critical path. The EFT of an activity is the earliest time by which an activity can finish without affecting the TPT or the logic of the network.
  An activity enters and finishes on the left-hand side of an event. If the event is the last event in the network, then the event represents the finish event of the network.
- The bottom right-hand quarter-segment contains the latest event time (LET) for that particular event which is the latest time at which the event can take place. The LET occurs at the same time as the:
  — Latest finishing time (LFT) of an activity, which is the latest time at which an activity can finish without affecting the TPT or the logic of the network.
  The LET also occurs at the same time as the:
  - Latest starting time (LST) of an activity when there is only one activity starting from the event or if the starting activity forms part of the critical path. The LST of an activity is the latest time by which an activity can start without affecting the TPT or the logic of the network.
  An activity leaves and starts on the right-hand side of an event. If the event is the first event in the network, then the event represents the start event of the network.

On occasion the physical size of the network may be restricted by the space available when constructing the diagram and also by the complexity of the relationships between the activities. In such a case, an activity arrow which finishes at, or starts from, an event can do so in an angled upwards or downwards direction leaning towards the right (e.g. activity *Fit rear lights* in Figure 12). The succeeding event should be drawn to the right of its preceding event so that the flow of time from left to right across the network is maintained.

---

1   There must be an event to denote the start of a network. The event which represents the start of the network is referred to as the **start event** of the network (sometimes referred to as the **opening event**, the **beginning event** or the **beginning node** of the network).

---

2   There must be an event to denote the finish of the network. The event which represents the finish of the network is referred to as the **finish event** of the network (sometimes referred to as the **closing event**, the **closing node** or the **end event** of the network).

3   An event which has more than one activity ending at it (i.e. entering it) and one or more activities subsequently starting from it (i.e. leaving it) is called a **merge node**.

4   An event which has one or more activities ending at it and more than one activity starting from it is called a **burst node**.

5   Any number of activities can enter the same **head event** as long as they do not share the same tail event (Chapter 2, Section 2.5).

6   The tail of an activity arrow leaves and starts from the **tail event** for that activity.

7   The head of an activity arrow enters and finishes at the head event for that activity.

8   An activity should not start before its **earliest starting time (EST)**.

9   An activity should not finish before its **earliest finishing time (EFT)**.

10 An activity should not start after its **latest starting time (LST)**.

11 An activity should not finish after its **latest finishing time (LFT)**.

2.5   Dummy activities

A dummy activity is used to maintain the logic of an Activity on Arrow (AoA) network and is pictorially defined as a dotted arrow, as shown in Figure 10. Unlike an activity, a dummy activity does not have a duration time nor does it use-up any resources.

Figure 10   An example of a dummy activity

In an Activity on Arrow network it is not permissible for two activities to start from the same preceding event and then enter the same succeeding event together as this would result in network ambiguity. An example of this form of network ambiguity is shown in Figure 11.

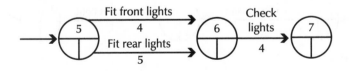

Figure 11   An example of network ambiguity

In Figure 11 activity *Fit front lights* and activity *Fit rear lights* cannot be drawn leaving the same preceding event and entering the same succeeding event. However, the restraints of the project require that activity *Check lights* does not start until activity *Fit front lights* and activity *Fit rear lights* have both been completed. Therefore, a dummy activity is drawn in the network so as to avoid ambiguity and to clarify that activity *Check lights* is dependent upon the prior completion of activity *Fit front lights* and activity *Fit rear lights*. Figure 12 shows how the network can be drawn correctly by the use of a dummy activity.

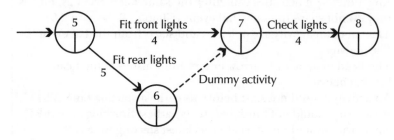

Figure 12 An example of the use of a dummy activity so as to retain the logic of the network

It is important to ensure that all events and activities are logically represented in the network. It is often the case that a particular event cannot take place until another specific event has already taken place (even through there may not be an activity to connect the two events). Figure 13 is part of an incorrectly drawn network which fails to show the requirement that event 9 be dependent upon the prior completion of event 8 (i.e. the start of activity *Check head lights* is dependent on the prior completion of activity *Fit wiring loom for head lights*).

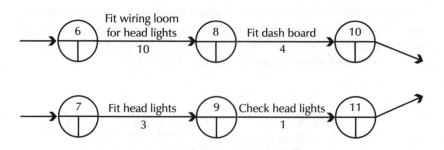

Figure 13 Part of a network prior to the inclusion of a dummy activity

To be able to start activity *Check head lights* it is necessary that activity *Fit wiring loom for head lights* and activity *Fit head lights* have already been completed. Therefore, the two parallel paths in the network are not entirely independent of each other. The dependence of event 9 on event 8 is defined correctly in Figure 14 by the use of a dummy activity which is drawn leading from the head event of activity *Fit wiring loom for head lights* to the tail event of activity *Check head lights*.

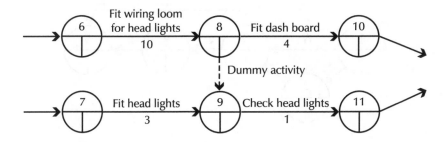

Figure 14 The part of a network shown in Figure 13, after the inclusion of a dummy activity

---

Dummy activities assist in the drawing of an Activity on Arrow network. They can be used to:

1 Prevent more than one activity from starting from the same **preceding event** and finishing at the same **succeeding event.**
2 Show that one or more activities is dependent upon other activities.

2.6 A comment on the drawing of dummy activities

Figures 15 and 16 show two methods of representing the dependency of a succeeding activity on a preceding activity by the use of a dummy activity. Either method of drawing a dummy activity is correct, but it is advisable to retain the same method throughout the network if possible.

Activity	Precedes activity
A	C, D
B	C, D
C	E
D	–
E	–

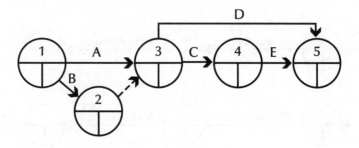

Figure 15 Drawing a dummy activity – Example 1

Activity	Preceding activity
A	–
B	–
C	A, B
D	A, B
E	C

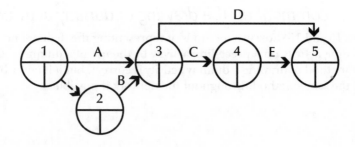

Figure 16 Drawing a dummy activity – Example 2

3 The Gantt chart

3.1 The Gantt chart

The Gantt chart was invented by Henry L. Gantt and graphically defines activities in terms of their duration time and the relationships between the activities. Gantt charts can be tailored to contain a wide variety of information (e.g. how much spare time an activity has), but care should be taken to ensure that the volume of information contained remains easily accessible to the user. A basic Gantt chart is shown as Figure 17.

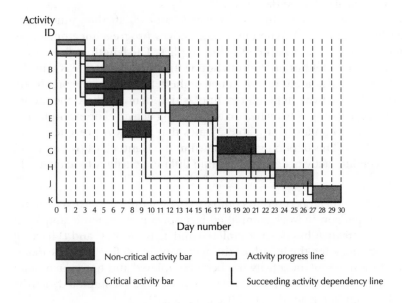

Figure 17 A basic Gantt chart

A Gantt chart consists of:

- A vertical axis, down which the activities of the project are listed from top to bottom.
- A horizontal axis, the length of which is proportionally divided into the unit used to define the duration time of the activities (e.g. days). Time

flows from left to right along the horizontal axis and starts at time 0 (e.g. 0 days).

- Dotted vertical guidelines, which act in conjunction with the horizontal axis, as a scaled framework within which the activity bars are sized in relation to their duration time.

- Horizontal non-critical activity bars (sometimes referred to as non-critical Gantt bars), each one of which represents a non-critical activity in the project. The length of a non-critical activity bar, in relation to divisions of the horizontal axis, represents the duration time of the activity. A non-critical activity bar is shaded dark grey in colour so as to distinguish it from critical activity bars which are shaded light grey.

- Horizontal critical activity bars (sometimes referred to as critical Gantt bars), each one of which represents a critical activity in the project. The length of a critical activity bar, in relation to the divisions of the horizontal axis, represents the duration time of the activity. A critical activity bar is shaded light grey so as to distinguish it from non-critical activity bars which are shaded dark grey.

- Activity progress line, which shows where appropriate, how much work has been completed. When used, the activity progress line appears inside the activity bar to which the line applies. The length of the activity progress line defines, in conjunction with the horizontal axis and the dotted vertical guidelines, how much of the activity has been completed.

- Succeeding activity dependency line, which denotes the dependency that a succeeding activity has on a preceding activity. For example, the information contained in Table 2 states that activity A precedes activities B, C, D. This dependency is shown in the Gantt chart by the use of a succeeding activity dependency line linking activity A to activities B, C, D.

A Gantt chart can be used to compare the scheduled progress of activities in comparison to work completed by a specific date. For example, in Figure 17, activity A has been completed and activities B, C and D have all started. By analysing the length of the activity progress line it can be determined how much of an activity has been completed and how much of an activity remains to be completed (e.g. activity B = 22% completed; activity C = 28% completed; activity D = 50% completed).

If necessary a Gantt chart can be drawn to depict the work status (e.g. an activity is behind schedule) at a specific date. This chart can then be compared with another Gantt chart which had been drawn at an earlier stage of the project before any of the activities had begun.

Another benefit of the Gantt chart is the way it displays that the start of the network is from time 0 (e.g. day 0). By working from day 0, the starting time and finishing time of an activity can be analysed in comparison to the numerical value of the days of work completed.

4 Activity on Arrow network logic

4.1 Examples of Activity on Arrow network logic

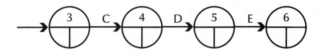

Figure 18   An example of sequential activities

Figure 18 shows three activities in sequence running along the same path. Activity C precedes activity D. Therefore, activity D cannot start until activity C has finished. Activity D precedes activity E and so activity D must finish before activity E can start.

Activity	Preceding activity
A	–
B	A
C	A
D	B
E	C
F	D
G	E

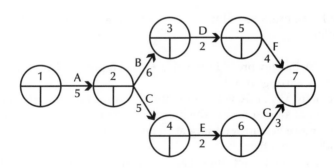

Figure 19   An example of sequential and parallel activities

- Activity A has no preceding activities in Figure 19. Event 1 has only activity A starting from it.
- When activity A finishes, activity B and activity C can start from event 2.
- Activity D cannot start until activity B ends. This is because activity D is dependent upon the prior completion of activity B.
- The start of activity E is dependent upon the prior completion of activity C.
- Activity F can start after activity D has finished.
- Activity G can start after activity E has been completed.

Activity	Precedes activity
A	B, C
B	D, E
C	E
D	F
E	G
F	–
G	–

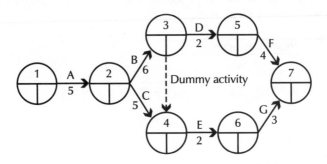

Figure 20   An example of the use of a dummy activity so as to maintain network logic

- Activity A has no preceding activities in Figure 20. Event 1 has only activity A starting from it.
- When activity A ends, activities B and C can start from event 2. Event 2 is known as a burst node, which is the term given to a node which has one or more activities ending at it, and more than one activity subsequently starting from it.
- Activity B precedes activities D and E. Therefore, activities D and E cannot start until activity B has finished. However, activity C must also precede activity E. Therefore, activity E cannot start until both activity B and activity C have finished. It is necessary to draw a dummy activity

between event 3 and event 4 so as to show that activity E is dependent on the prior completion of activity B. It is not possible to draw a solid activity arrow because no identity could be given to the activity that would be thus drawn into the network.
- Activity D precedes activity F. Activity F has no succeeding activity.
- Activity E precedes activity G. Activity G has no succeeding activity.

---

1   All activities have a **unique identity**.
2   A burst node is the term given to a node which has one or more activities ending at it and more than one activity subsequently starting from it.

Activity	Precedes activity
A	B, C
B	D
C	D, E
D	F
E	G
F	–
G	–

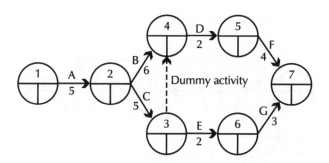

Figure 21   An example of the use of a dummy activity so as to maintain network logic

- Activity A has no preceding activities in Figure 21. Event 1 has only activity A starting from it.
- Activity A precedes activities B and C. Once activity A has finished, activities B and C can start.
- Activity B precedes activity D. Therefore, activity B must be completed before activity D can start. However, activity C also precedes activity D (activity C must also precede activity E). Therefore, activity D cannot

21

start until activities B and C have been completed. It is necessary to draw a dummy activity between event 3 and event 4 so as to ensure a logical sequence in the network. The dummy activity between event 3 and event 4 denotes that activity D is dependent upon the prior completion of activity C. It is not possible to draw a solid activity arrow because no identity could be given to the activity which would be drawn into the network.

- Activity F can start after activity D has been completed.
- Activity G can start after activity E has finished.

---

1   The events in the network of Figure 21 have been numbered in an order referred to as **sequential numbering**. Sequential numbering requires that a succeeding event has a higher unique event number than an event which the succeeding event succeeds.

Activity	Precedes activity
A	C, D
B	C, D
C	E
D	F
E	F
F	–

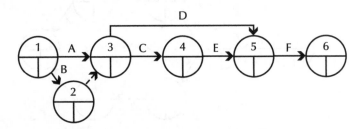

Figure 22   An example of the use of a dummy activity so as to maintain network logic

- Activities A and B have no preceding activities in Figure 22. Activities A and B, and the event from which they start, represent the start of the network.
- Activities A and B precede activities C and D. The network would be incorrectly drawn if both activities A and B were shown starting from the same preceding event and entering the same succeeding event together (as shown in Figure 23). The dummy activity is added to the network in Figure 22 so as to correctly show the dependence that activities C and D have on the prior completion of activities A and B.

- Activity C precedes activity E. When activity C has finished, activity E can start.
- Activity F is dependent upon the prior completion of activity D and activity E. The completion of activity F results in the finish of the network.

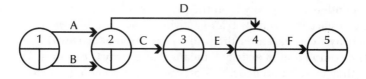

Figure 23   The network shown in Figure 22, but drawn incorrectly

Activity	Preceding activity
A	–
B	–
C	A
D	B
E	B, C
F	D
G	E

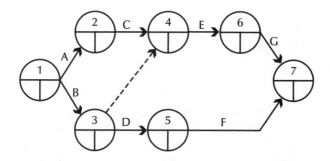

Figure 24   An example of the use of a dummy activity so as to maintain network logic

- Activities A and B represent the start of the network in Figure 24 because they are shown in the table of activities as having no preceding activities (this is shown by the symbol –).
- The start of activity C is dependent upon the completion of preceding activity A.

- The start of activity D is dependent upon the completion of preceding activity B.
- The start of activity E is dependent upon the prior completion of activities B and C. A dummy activity is drawn from the head event of activity B (i.e. event 3 at which activity B finishes) to the tail event of activity E (i.e. event 4 from which activity E starts). This dummy activity shows the dependence of activity E on the prior completion of activity B. Activity E can start after activity B and activity C have both finished.
- Activity F can start after the prior completion of activity D.
- The completion of activity E means that activity G can start.
- Both activity F and activity G precede no succeeding activities and so the head event into which these two activities enter represents the finish event of the network.

---

1   In Figure 24, it would not be possible to draw a solid activity arrow from the head event of activity B to the tail event of activity E, because this would create an activity which would have neither a unique identity or a duration time.

Activity	Preceding activity
A	–
B	–
C	A
D	B, C
E	C
F	D
G	E

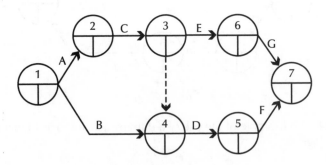

Figure 25   An example of the use of a dummy activity so as to maintain network logic

- Activities A and B represent the start of the network in Figure 25 because they are shown in the table of activities as having no preceding activities.
- The start of activity C is dependent upon the prior completion of activity A.
- The table of activities states that the start of activity D is dependent upon the completion of activity B and activity C. A dummy activity is drawn leading from the head event of activity C (i.e. event 3) and entering into the tail event of activity D (i.e. event 4). This dummy activity denotes that the start of activity D is dependent upon the prior completion of activity C. Activity D can start once activity B and activity C have both finished.
- The start of activity F is dependent upon the prior completion of preceding activity D.
- The start of activity G is dependent upon the completion of activity E.
- Both activity F and activity G precede no succeeding activities and so the head event into which these two activities enter represents the finish of the network.

Activity	Preceding activity
A	–
B	–
C	–
D	A, B
E	A, C
F	D, E

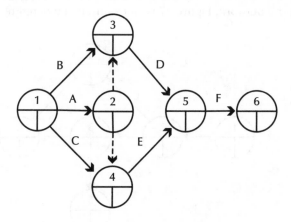

Figure 26 An example of the use of a dummy activity so as to maintain network logic

25

- Activities A, B and C represent the start of the network in Figure 26.
- The start of activity D is dependent upon the prior completion of activities A and B. Activity E is also dependent upon the completion of activity A (as well as being dependent upon the prior completion of activity C). It is important to show the dependency of activities D and E on the prior completion of activity A (while maintaining the relevant dependency on either activity B or activity C). This is achieved through the use of two dummy activities, both of which start from event 2 which represents the finish of activity A. One dummy activity starts from event 2 and ends at event 3 (i.e. the tail event for activity D), the other dummy activity starts at event 2 and ends at event 4 (i.e. the tail event for activity E).
- Once activities A and B have been completed, activity D can start.
- Once activities A and C have been completed, activity E can start.
- The completion of activities D and E at event 5 means that activity F can start. Event 5 is referred to as a merge node, which is the term given to a node which has more than one activity ending at it, and one or more activities subsequently starting from it. The completion of activity F represent the finish of the network.

4.2   Dangling activity

A dangling activity can occur when an activity, when completed, enters an event which represents neither the start point of another activity or the finish of the network and thus the completion of the project. To avoid the occurrence of a dangling activity, it is important to ensure that the description of an activity does not cause ambiguity. However, it is more often than not that a dangling activity will be caused simply through oversight while drawing the network. Figure 27 is an example of a dangling activity.

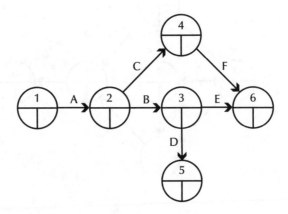

Figure 27   An example of a dangling activity

In Figure 27, activity D enters event 5 which represents neither the start point of another activity nor the finish of the network. As a result activity D and event 5 have no logical contribution towards the completion of the network. Event 6 denotes the finish of the network because the sequential numbering of the events denotes that event 6 occurs after event 5.

Network logic states that:

1   It is only in complex networks, which contain multiple starts and finishes, that an activity can appear to dangle. Such networks are beyond the scope of this book.
2   Apart from the start event, all events will have at least one activity which will enter and finish at the event.
3   Apart from the finish event of a network, all events will have at least one activity which will leave and start from the event.

4.3   Looping

Looping occurs when an error is made while drawing the network. This results in a group of activities being dependent upon each other on a constantly re-occurring basis so that a preceding activity becomes dependent upon a succeeding activity and a preceding event becomes dependent upon a succeeding event. Such a dependency is shown in Figure 28.

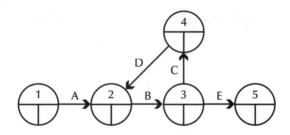

Figure 28   An example of looping within a network

In Figure 28:

• Activity B is dependent upon activity A and activity D.
• Activity C is dependent upon activity B.
• Activity D is dependent upon activity C.
• Activity B is then again dependent upon activity A and activity D.
   The network denotes that event 3 occurs after event 2 and event 4 oc-

curs after event 3, which is logical. However, event 2 is shown to occur after event 4. This loop is illogical.

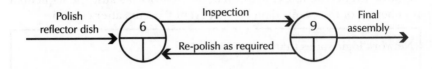

Figure 29   An incorrect example of a cycle of activities

The network in Figure 29 indicates that activity *Final assembly* cannot start until the reflector dish has been polished until it passes *Inspection*. In order to prevent such a cycle of activities, activity *Inspection* and activity *Re-polish as required* are grouped together so that they are depicted in the network as one activity (i.e. *Inspect and re-polish as required*), as shown in Figure 30.

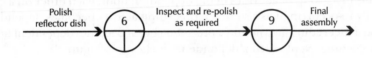

Figure 30   The logical representation of a cycle of activities

5 The forward pass and the backward pass in an AoA network

5.1 The forward pass in an AoA network

The forward pass involves the calculation of the earliest starting time (EST) of each activity in the network. The process of the forward pass determines the total project time (TPT). The formula for calculating the EST of an activity is:

> **EST of activity 'X' = EST of preceding activity + its duration time**

Figure 31 shows that activity H, which starts from event 6, is dependent upon the prior completion of preceding activity E. Therefore, the EST for activity H is 12 minutes (7 + 5 = 12). The EST of activity H is also the earliest finishing time (EFT) for activity E. The formula for calculating the EFT of an activity is:

> **EFT of activity 'X' = EST of activity 'X' + its duration time**

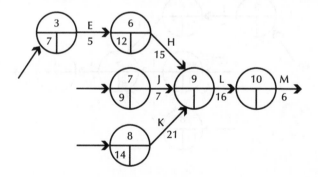

Figure 31 Activity H and its dependency on activity E

Now, assume that activities H, J, K and L represent 4 trains. Train L cannot leave until trains H, J and K have arrived at event 9, from which train L will leave. Therefore, the EST for train L is determined by the train which will finish the latest at event 9. The duration time of trains H, J and K are shown in Table 4.

Table 4 The duration times for trains H, J and K

Activity (train)	Duration time (in minutes)
H	15
J	7
K	21

By using the formula for determining the EST of an activity, it can be calculated that the EST for train L, and thus the earliest event time (EET) for event 9, is 35 minutes (14 + 21 = 35). This is because train K has the latest EFT out of the trains which finish at event 9. The calculation for the EST of train L is shown in Table 5.

Table 5 Table of calculations for the EST of train L

Activity (train)	Calculations	EST (minutes)
H	12 + 15 =	27
J	9 + 7 =	16
K	14 + 21 =	35

The EST of 35 minutes for train L is displayed in the lower left quarter segment of event 9. This EST of 35 minutes for train L is also the EET for event 9, as shown in Figure 32.

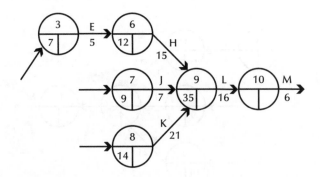

Figure 32 Network showing the EST for train L and the EET for event 9

To calculate the EST of train M (and thus the EET of Event 10, and coincidentally the EFT of train L) it is necessary to add together the EST of train L and its duration time (35 + 16 = 51 minutes). Figure 33 shows the

EST of train M (and the EET for event 10 and the EFT of train L) displayed in the lower left quarter segment of event 10.

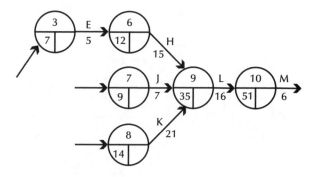

Figure 33   The EST for train M

5.2   The backward pass in an AoA network

The purpose of the backward pass is to determine the latest time by which all activities finish at an event without affecting the TPT. Therefore, the backward pass determines the latest finishing time (LFT) of an activity and the latest event time (LET) of the event. The LFT of an activity can be calculated using the following formula:

LFT of activity 'X' = LFT of succeeding activity – its duration time

---

The backward pass also determines the latest starting time (LST) of an activity. The LST of an activity can be calculated using the following formula:

LST of activity 'X' = LFT of activity 'X' – its duration time

---

The finish event of the network (sometimes called the closing event or closing node of the network) is used as the start point when performing the backward pass. All calculations of the backward pass are made while progressively moving from right to left across the network until the last calculation has been performed at the start event of the network.

In Figure 34, event 21 is the finish event of the network. The EET by which the project can be completed (i.e. the TPT) is shown in the left-hand quarter segment of event 21 as being 98 days. If the project is to be completed on time, the LET for event 21 is also 98 days, which is shown in the right-hand quarter segment. To determine the LFT of activities M, L and K and the LET of events 20, 19 and 18 (and coincidentally the LST of

31

activities Q, P and N) the duration time of activities Q, P and N are individually deducted from the LFT of activities Q, P and N. These calculations are shown in Table 6.

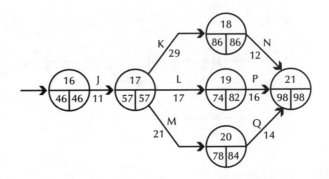

Figure 34 Network showing the LST/LET

Table 6 The LFT of activities M, L and K

Activity	Calculations	LFT (minutes)
M	98 – 14 =	84
L	98 – 16 =	82
K	98 – 12 =	86

It will often be the case that an event will have more than one activity starting from it. In Figure 34, event 17 has three activities starting from it (i.e. activities K, L and M). The LET of event 17 is determined by the activity with the earliest LST out of those activities which start from event 17. Calculation of the LET for event 17 is as follows:

- LST of activity M = 63 days (84 – 21 = 63).
- LST of activity L = 65 days (82 – 17 = 65).
- LST of activity K = 57 days (86 – 29 = 57).

The LET for event 17 is 57 days because this is the LST by which activity K can successfully start and subsequently finish by its LFT of 86 days (57 + 29 = 86). As a result, activity J must finish by day 57 so as not to disrupt the LET of event 17.

The LET of event 16, and coincidentally the LST of activity J (because activity J is the only activity starting from event 16), is calculated by subtracting the duration time of activity J from its LFT ($57 - 11 = 46$ days). Through analysis of the backward pass the critical path of the network can be identified (Chapter 6).

- The acronym for the earliest starting time is EST.
- The acronym for the earliest finishing time is EFT.
- The acronym for the **earliest event time** is **EET**.
- The EST of activity 'X' = EST of preceding activity + its duration time.
- The EFT of activity 'X' = EST of activity 'X' + its duration time.
- Where more than one activity finishes at an event, the EET of the event (and therefore the EST of any succeeding activity which starts from the event) is determined by the preceding activity which finishes latest at the event.
- The forward pass determines the EST of an activity and the total project time (TPT).
- The acronym for the latest starting time is LST.
- The acronym for the latest finishing time is LFT.
- The acronym for the **latest event time** is **LET**.
- The LST of activity 'X' = LFT of activity 'X' – its duration time.
- The LFT of activity 'X' = LFT of succeeding activity – its duration time.
- Where more than one activity starts from an event, the LET of the event (and therefore the LFT of any activities which finish at the event) is determined by the activity which starts the earliest from the event.
- The backward pass determines the LFT of an activity and assists identification of the location of the critical path of the network

---

5.3 Example 1 – A worked example of a forward pass for network A

Table 7 lists the activities and duration times of network A, Figure 35, which represent a project concerning the manufacture, inspection, assembly and testing of the prototype for a new consumer appliance.

Table 7   Table of activities for network A

Activity	Description	Preceding activity	Duration*
A	Release drawings, tooling, raw materials and bought-out electro-plated components	–	3
B	Machine required components from raw materials	A	9
C	Fabricate sheet-metal components from raw materials	A	7
D	Polish machined components which are not to be electro-plated	B	5
E	Electro-plate machined components which require plating	B	4
F	Stove enamel fabricated components	C	3
G	Inspect polished machined components	D	4
H	Inspect all electro-plated components	A, E	3
J	Inspect stove enamelled components	F	7
K	Assemble prototype from components then test	G, H, J	4

* Duration time in days.

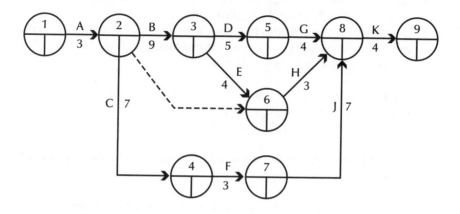

Figure 35   Network A before the forward pass

The forward pass for network A, Figure 35, is as follows:

5.3.1   The forward pass for network A (AoA method)

Calculations involved in the forward pass make use of the following formula:

> **EST of activity 'X' = EST of preceding activity + its duration time**

- Event 1 has an EET of 0 days which is assigned to the event. Activity A starts at day 0.
- Event 2 has an EET of 3 days $(0 + 3 = 3)$ which is assigned to the event. Activities B and C can start at day 3.
- Event 3 has an EET of 12 days $(3 + 9 = 12)$ which is assigned to the event. Activities D and E can start at day 12.
- Event 4 has an EET of 10 days $(3 + 7 = 10)$ which is assigned to the event. Activity F can start at day 10.
- Event 5 has an EET of 17 days $(12 + 5 = 17)$ which is assigned to the event. Activity G can start at day 17.
- Event 6 has an EET of 16 days $(12 + 4 = 16)$. This is because the only other activity that ends at event 6 is a dummy activity which forms a chain of activities with activity A. The dummy activity is required so as to show that activity H is dependent upon the prior completion of activity A. This chain has a combined duration time of 3 days $(0 + 3 + 0 = 3)$. Activity H can start at day 16. The EET for event 6 is assigned to the event.

35

- Event 7 has an EET of 13 days (10 + 3 = 13) which is assigned to the event. As a result activity J can start at day 13.
- Event 8 has three activities finishing at it. The EET of event 8 is determined by the latest EFT of the activities which lead into this event. The calculation for event 8 is as follows:

  - EFT of activity G = 21 days (17 + 4 = 21).
  - EFT of activity H = 19 days (16 + 3 = 19).
  - EFT of activity J = 20 days (13 + 7 = 20).

  The EET for event 8 is 21 days which is assigned to the event. Activity K can start at day 21.

- Event 9 has an EET of 25 days (21 + 4 = 25) which is assigned to the event. Event 9 represents the finish event of network A.

> **The minimum amount of time required to complete the project is 25 days. Therefore, the TPT for network A is 25 days.**

The completed forward pass for network A is shown as Figure 36.

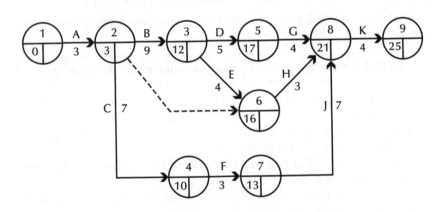

Figure 36 Network A with the forward pass completed

The EET calculations for Network A, Figure 36, are shown in tabulated form in Table 8.

Table 8   The EET calculations for network A

Event	Calculations	EET (days)
1	0 + 0 =	0
2	0 + 3 =	3
3	3 + 9 =	12
4	3 + 7 =	10
5	12 + 5 =	17
6	12 + 4 =	16
7	10 + 3 =	13
8	17 + 4 =	21
9	21 + 4 =	25

The backward pass for network A is as follows:

5.3.2   The backward pass for network A (AoA method)

Calculations involved in the backward pass make use of the following formula:

LST of activity 'X' = LFT of activity 'X' – its duration time

---

- If the TPT of 25 days is to be observed the LET for event 9 will be 25 days.
- Event 8 has an LET of 21 days (25 – 4 = 21) which is assigned to the event. Activities G, H and J must finish by day 21 if activity K is to start by its LST.
- Event 7 has an LET of 14 days (21 – 7 = 14) which is assigned to the event. Activity F must finish by day 14 if activity J is to start by its LST.
- Event 6 has an LET of 18 days (21 – 3 = 18) which is assigned to the event. Activity E must finish by day 18 if activity H is to start by its LST.
- Event 5 has an LET of 17 days (21 – 4 = 17) which is assigned to the event. Activity D must finish by day 17 if activity G is to start by its LST.
- Event 4 has an LET of 11 days (14 – 3 = 11) which is assigned to the event. Activity C must finish by day 11 if activity F is to start by its LST.
- Event 3 has two activities starting from it. The LET of event 3 is determined by the earliest LST of the activities which start from event 3. The calculation for the LET of event 3 is as follows:
  - LST of activity E = 14 days (18 – 4 = 14).
  - LST of activity D = 12 days (17 – 5 = 12).
  The LET for event 3 is 12 days which is assigned to the event. Activity B must finish by day 12 if activity D is to start by its LST.

- Event 2 has activities B and C starting from it, and a dummy activity which represents the dependency of activity H on the prior completion of activity A. The LET of event 2 is determined by the earliest LST of the activities which start from that event. The calculation for the LET of event 2 is as follows:
  - LST of activity C = 4 days (11 – 7 = 4).
  - LST of activity B = 3 days (12 – 9 = 3).
  - LST of dummy activity = 18 days (18 – 0 = 18).

  The LET for event 2 is 3 days which is assigned to the event. Activity A must finish by day 3 if activity B is to start by its LST.
- Event 1 has an LET of 0 days (3 – 3 = 0). The LET for event 1 is assigned to the event.

The completed backward pass for network A is shown as Figure 37.

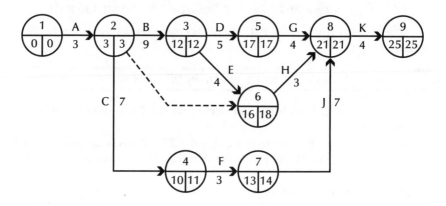

Figure 37   Network A with the backward pass completed

The LET calculations for network A in Figure 37 are shown in tabulated form in Table 9.

Table 9   The LET calculations for network A

Event	Calculations	LET (days)
8	25 – 4 =	21
7	21 – 7 =	14
6	21 – 3 =	18
5	21 – 4 =	17
4	14 – 3 =	11
3	17 – 5 =	12
2	12 – 9 =	3
1	3 – 3 =	0

The EST, LST, EFT, LFT for the activities of network A are summarised in Table 10.

Table 10   A summary table of the duration time, EST, LST, EFT and LFT for the activities of network A

Activity	Duration (days)	Start		Finish	
		EST	LST	EFT	LFT
A	3	0	0	3	3
B	9	3	3	12	12
C	7	3	4	10	11
D	5	12	12	17	17
E	4	12	14	16	18
F	3	10	11	13	14
G	4	17	17	21	21
H	3	16	18	19	21
J	7	13	14	20	21
K	4	21	21	25	25

EFT of activity = EST of activity + duration time of activity
LST of activity = LFT of activity – duration time of activity

5.3.3   Caution when considering the LST and EFT of an activity (in comparison to the network defined LET and the EET)

Network A, Figure 37, denotes that the EET of the tail event from which activity E starts (i.e. event 3) is 12 days and that the EST of activity E is also 12 days. The network also denotes that the LET for event 3 is 12 days. However, this LET of 12 days is not equal to the LST of activity E. If the

LET of 12 days for event 3 is subtracted from the LET of 18 days for event 6, at which activity E finishes, the resulting time available to complete activity E is 6 days ($18 - 12 = 6$). However, activity E has a duration time of only 4 days. This means that activity E will have an LST of 14 days ($18 - 4 = 14$). This difference between the LET of event 3 and the LST of activity E is due to the LET of event 3 being dictated by activity D, which has the earliest LST of any activity which starts from event 3 (i.e. 12 days). It should be noted that the LST of an activity is only equal to the LET of the tail event from which the activity starts, if this activity is the only activity to start from the event or if the activity forms part of the critical path. Therefore, it is important to ensure when considering the LST value of an activity, that the LST time relates to the activity time and not necessarily the event time of the tail event from which the activity starts.

It is of equal importance to ensure that the EFT value relates to the activity and not necessarily the EET value of the head event at which the activity finishes. For example, the EET of event 8 is 21 days. However, the EFT of activity J is 20 days ($13 + 7 = 20$). The EET of event 8 is dictated by the EFT of activity G ($17 + 4 = 21$). It should be noted that the EFT of an activity is only equal to the EET of the head event at which the activity finishes, if this activity is the only activity to finish at the event or if the activity forms part of the critical path.

5.4   The EET/LET matrix method of calculating the EET and LET

5.4.1   The elements of an EET/LET matrix

The EET/LET matrix provides a method of calculating and displaying event times. An example of an EET/LET matrix is shown as Figure 38.

| | Succeeding event number | | | | | | | | | |
	1	2	3	4	5	6	7	8	9	EET cell
1		3								0
2			9	7		0				3
3					5	4				12
4							3			10
5								4		17
6								3		16
7								7		13
8									4	21
9										25
LET cell	0	3	12	11	17	18	14	21	25	

Preceding event number (vertical axis label on left)

The inter-connecting duration time cell for events 7 and 8

Figure 38   The EET/LET matrix

- Preceding event numbers are inserted, in ascending order down the left-hand side of the matrix.
- Succeeding event numbers are inserted, in ascending order from left to right across the top of the matrix.
- The EET for each event is inserted, in ascending order in the appropriate EET Cell, in the column down the right-hand side of the matrix.
- The LET for each event is inserted, in ascending order in the appropriate LET Cell, in the row running across the bottom of the matrix.
- The duration time of an activity that links a preceding event and a succeeding event is inserted in the inter-connecting duration time cell which occurs at the inter-connection between the horizontal axis of the preceding event, and the vertical axis of the succeeding event.

- A diagonal line is drawn from the top-left to the bottom-right of the matrix. Any cell through which the diagonal line passes is called a diagonal cell. When sequential event numbering is used, the duration times will appear in the duration time cells above the diagonal line.

The completion of an EET/LET matrix consists of:

1 The insertion of the activity duration times into the duration time cells.
2 The forward pass, so as to determine the EET of each event and the TPT.
3 The backward pass, so as to determine the LET of each event and the critical path.

The following example concerns the completion of an EET/LET matrix for network A. The table of activities for network A is shown as table 11; the construction of network A is pictorially defined in Figure 39.

Table 11 The table of activities for network A

	Activity	Preceding activity	Duration*
Opening	A	–	3
	B	A	9
	C	A	7
	D	B	5
	E	B	4
	F	C	3
	G	D	4
	H	A, E	3
	J	F	7
Closing	K	G, H, J	4

* Duration time in days.

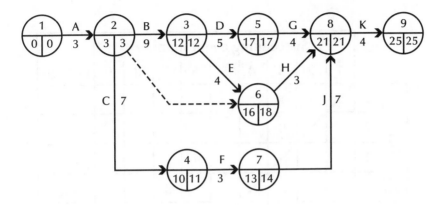

Figure 39 Network A

5.4.2 Insertion of activity duration times

1. Start at the preceding event number for the event from which the activity will start.
2. Move horizontally along the row of cells, which leads from the preceding event number, until reaching the inter-connecting duration time cell which inter-connects with the vertical column containing the succeeding event number.
3. Insert, into the inter-connecting duration time cell, the duration time of the activity.
4. Repeat this process until all activity duration times have been inserted.

The EET/LET matrix, with the activity duration times for network A inserted, is shown as Figure 40.

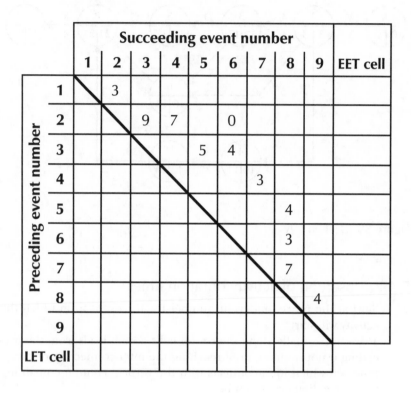

Figure 40 The EET/LET matrix for network A with activity duration times inserted

It should be noted that if the network contains events which do not occur in sequence, the duration time of the activity that joins two events will be shown in a duration time cell below the diagonal line.

5.4.3 The forward pass (EET/LET matrix method) for network A

1 Because there is no preceding activity before event 1, event 1 has an EET of day 0. Insert the EET for event 1 (i.e. 0) in the EET cell for this event.

2 Start at preceding event 2 situated on the left-hand side of the matrix. Move horizontally to the right along the row of cells which leads from event 2 until reaching the cell within which the diagonal line appears.

From the diagonal cell, move vertically upwards through the column in which this particular diagonal cell occurs until a duration time is reached in one of the duration time cells within the column.

When a duration time is located (in this case a duration time of 3 days), it then moves horizontally, from this duration time cell, across the row of cells to the EET cell on the far right-hand side of this row.

Add the duration time which has been noted to the EET shown in the EET cell to give the EET for event 2 (in this case $0 + 3 = 3$). Insert the calculated EET into the EET cell at the far right of the row which begins with preceding event 2.

3   Event 3; move horizontally to the right to the diagonal line cell, then move vertically upwards to an occupied duration cell. Note the duration time (9 days). Move horizontally to the right to the EET cell on the far right of row. Add the duration time which has been noted to the EET shown in the EET cell to give the EET for event 3 ($3 + 9 = 12$ days). Insert the EET for event 3 in the EET cell for this event.

4   Event 4; move horizontally to the right to the diagonal line cell, then move vertically upwards to an occupied duration cell. Note the duration time (7 days). Move horizontally to the right to the EET cell on the far right of row. Add the duration time which has been noted to the EET shown in the EET cell to give the EET for event 4 ($3 + 7 = 10$ days). Insert the EET for event 4 in the EET cell for this event.

5   Event 5; move horizontally to the right to the diagonal line cell, then move vertically upwards to an occupied duration cell. Note the duration time (5 days). Move horizontally to the right to the EET cell on the far right of row. Add the duration time which has been noted to the EET shown in the EET cell to give the EET for event 5 ($12 + 5 = 17$ days). Insert the EET for event 5 in the EET cell for this event.

6   Event 6 requires that more than one calculation be performed because there is more than one duration time in the column leading vertically upwards from the diagonal line cell. Move horizontally to the right to the diagonal line cell, then move vertically upwards to an occupied duration cell. Note the duration time (4 days). Move horizontally to the right to the EET cell on the far right of row. Add the duration time which has been noted to the EET shown in the EET cell to give a possible EET for event 6 ($12 + 4 = 16$). Repeat this process until all the duration times within the column have been accounted for. The calculations are as follows:

- $12 + 4 = 16$ days.
- $3 + 0 = 3$ days.

The EET for event 6 is dependent upon the latest EFT of any of the activities which finish at this event. Therefore, the EET for event 6 is 16 days (12 + 4 = 16 days). Insert the EET for event 6 in the EET cell for this event.

7   Event 7; move horizontally to the right to the diagonal line cell, then move vertically upwards to an occupied duration cell. Note the duration time (3 days). Move horizontally to the right to the EET cell on the far right of row. Add the duration time which has been noted to the EET shown in the EET cell to give the EET for event 7 (10 + 3 = 13 days). Insert the EET for event 7 in the EET cell for this event.

8   Event 8; move horizontally to the right to the diagonal line cell, then move vertically upwards to an occupied duration cell. Note the duration time. Move horizontally to the right to the EET cell on the far right of row. Add the duration time which has been noted to the EET shown in the EET cell to give a possible EET for event 8. Repeat this process until all duration times within the column have been accounted for. The calculations are as follows:

- 13 + 7 = 20 days.
- 16 + 3 = 19 days.
- 17 + 4 = 21 days.

The EET for event 8 is 21 days (17 + 4 = 21 days) because this is the latest EFT of any activity which finishes at event 8. Insert the EET for event 8 in the EET cell for this event.

9   Event 9; move horizontally to the right to the diagonal line cell, then move vertically upwards to an occupied duration cell. Note the duration time (4 days). Move horizontally to the right to the EET cell on the far right of row. Add the duration time which has been noted to the EET shown in the EET cell to give the EET for event 9 (21 + 4 = 25 days). Insert the EET for event 9 in the EET cell for this event.

The EET/LET matrix, with the forward pass completed for Network A, is shown as Figure 41.

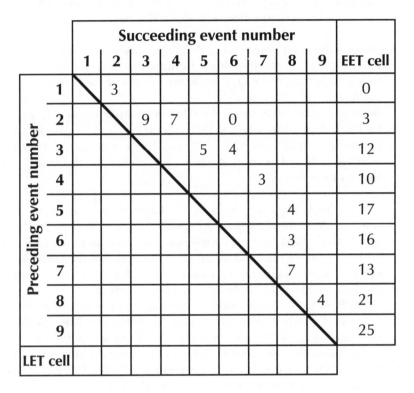

Figure 41   The EET/LET matrix with the forward pass complete

5.4.4   The backward pass (EET/LET matrix method) for network A

1   Because event 9 is the closing event of the network, the EET of event 9 is also the LET for event 9. Insert the LET for event 9 (in this case 25 days) in the LET cell for this event.

2   Start at the second from last succeeding event number located at the top of the matrix (for network A the second from last event will be event 8). Move vertically down the column of cells which lead from event 8 until reaching the cell within which the diagonal line appears.

From the diagonal cell, move horizontally to the right along the row within which the diagonal cell occurs until a duration time is reached in one of the duration time cells within this row.

When a duration time is located (in this case 4 days), note it, then move vertically down the column within which the cell with the duration time occurs to the LET cell at the bottom of the matrix.

Subtract the duration time, which has been already noted, from the LET cell time value shown in the relevant LET cell to give the LET for event 8 (in this case 25 – 4 = 21 days). Insert the calculated LET into the LET cell at the bottom of the column which begins with succeeding event 8.

3   Event 7; move vertically down to the diagonal line cell, then move horizontally to the right to an occupied duration cell. Note the duration time (7 days). Move vertically down the column to the LET cell at the bottom of the column. Subtract the duration time from LET cell time value to give the LET for event 7 (21 – 7 = 14 days). Insert the LET for event 7 into the LET cell for this event.

4   Event 6; move vertically down to the diagonal line cell, then move horizontally to the right to an occupied duration cell. Note the duration time (3 days). Move vertically down the column to the LET cell at the bottom of the column. Subtract the duration time from LET cell time value to give the LET for event 6 (21 – 3 = 18 days). Insert the LET for event 6 into the LET cell for this event.

5   Event 5; move vertically down to the diagonal line cell, then move horizontally to the right to an occupied duration cell. Note the duration time (4 days). Move vertically down the column to the LET cell at the bottom of the column. Subtract the duration time from LET cell time value to give the LET for event 6 (21 – 4 = 17 days). Insert the LET for event 5 into the LET cell for this event.

6   Event 4; move vertically down to the diagonal line cell, then move horizontally to the right to an occupied duration cell. Note the duration time (3 days). Move vertically down the column to the LET cell at the bottom of the column. Subtract the duration time from LET cell time value to give the LET for event 4 (14 – 3 = 11 days). Insert the LET for event 4 into the LET cell for this event.

7   Event 3 requires that more than one calculation be performed because there is more than one duration time located in the row leading across from the diagonal line cell. Move vertically down to the diagonal line cell, then move horizontally to the right to an occupied duration cell. Note the duration time. Move vertically down the column to the LET cell at the bottom of the column. Subtract the dura-

tion time from the LET cell time value to give a possible LET for event 3. Repeat this process until all the duration times within the row have been accounted for. The calculations are as follows:

- $17 - 5 = 12$ days.
- $18 - 4 = 14$ days.

The LET for Event 3 is dependent upon the earliest LST of any of the activities which start from this event. Therefore, the LET for event 3 is 12 days ($17 - 5 = 12$ days). Insert the LET for event 3 into the LET cell for this event.

8   Event 2, move vertically down to the diagonal line cell, then move horizontally to the right to an occupied duration cell. Note the duration time. Move vertically down the column to the LET cell at the bottom of the column. Subtract the duration time from the LET cell time value to give a possible LET for event 2. Repeat this process until all the duration times within the row have been accounted for. The calculations are as follows:

- $12 - 9 = 3$ days.
- $11 - 7 = 4$ days.
- $18 - 0 = 18$ days.

The LET for event 2 is 3 days ($12 - 9 = 3$ days). Insert the LET for event 2 into the LET cell for this event.

9   Event 1, move vertically down to the diagonal line cell, then move horizontally to the right to an occupied duration cell. Note the duration time (3 days). Move vertically down the column to the LET cell at the bottom of the column. Subtract the duration time from LET cell time value to give the LET for event 2 ($3 - 3 = 0$ days). Insert the LET for event 1 into the LET cell for this event.

The critical path occurs through those events where the EET and LET of an event have the same value (i.e. the critical path occurs through events 1, 2, 3, 5, 8 and 9). The EET/LET matrix, with the backward pass completed for network A, is shown as Figure 42.

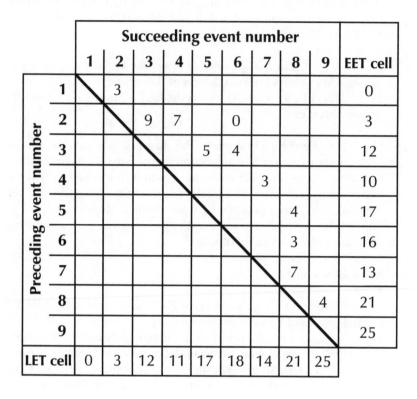

		\multicolumn{9}{c}{**Succeeding event number**}	
		1	**2**	**3**	**4**	**5**	**6**	**7**	**8**	**9**	**EET cell**
Preceding event number	**1**		3								0
	2			9	7		0				3
	3					5	4				12
	4							3			10
	5								4		17
	6								3		16
	7								7		13
	8									4	21
	9										25
LET cell		0	3	12	11	17	18	14	21	25	

Figure 42   The EET/LET matrix with the backward pass complete

6 The critical path in an AoA network

6.1 The critical path in an AoA network

The path of activities (sometimes called the chain of activities), through the network which determines the overall time required to complete the project is called the critical path. The critical path is depicted in an Activity on Arrow (AoA) network by drawing two lines across the shaft of each arrow which represent an activity that lies along the critical path. The activities which occur along the critical path are referred to as critical activities. Any delay in the completion of a critical activity (i.e. if any critical activity does not start at its earliest starting time (EST) and does not finish by its earliest finishing time (EFT) will cause a delay in the finish of the project. It is possible for a network to contain more than one critical path if the relevant paths possess the same longest time to complete.

> The critical path for network A occurs through activities A, B, D, G and K (i.e. events 1, 2, 3, 5, 8 and 9) and is shown in Figure 43.

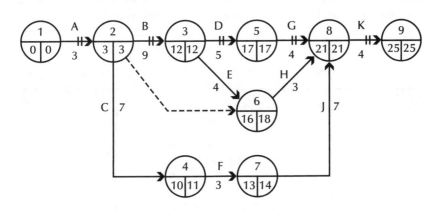

Figure 43 Network A with the critical path defined

The critical path can often be identified by the path of activities which have the most minimal spare time (i.e. the nearest to zero spare time).

This spare time is nominally referred to as float. It will often be the case that the critical path will occur along those activities where the EET and the LET of each event will be the same. HOWEVER, THIS IS NOT AL-WAYS THE CASE, AND IT IS IMPORTANT TO SHOW CAUTION WHEN ASSIGNING THE CRITICAL PATH (Section 6.3).

---

1   The critical path lies along the path of activities which determines the overall time required to complete the project. The activities which occur along the critical path will have minimal spare time (this spare time is nominally referred to as float) and are referred to as critical activities.

2   The overall duration time is equivalent to the minimum overall time required to complete the project. This minimum overall time is referred to as the total project time (TPT).

3   It is possible for a network to contain more than one critical path if the relevant paths possess the same longest time to complete.

6.2   Crashing the critical path

So far the analysis of CPA in this book has covered the planning and control of a project before it has begun and not during the life-cycle of the project where some activities may be required to be completed within a reduced duration time. Crashing is the process of shortening the length of the critical path (i.e. the TPT is reduced) by reducing the duration time of activities which occur along the critical path. The following example of crashing the critical path relates to Figure 44, network A.

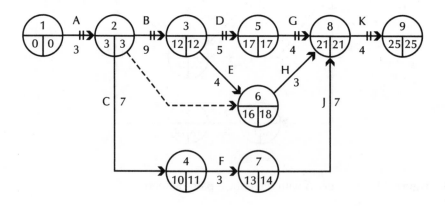

Figure 44   Network A

52

6.2.1 The scenario concerning the crashing of network A

The critical path of network A, Figure 44, runs through activities A, B, D, G and K (i.e. events 1, 2, 3, 5, 8 and 9). Senior management are concerned about the costs of the project and have ordered that a study be undertaken to see if the TPT of 25 days can be reduced. Analysis of the processes undertaken during each of the activities has resulted in a re-evaluation of the duration times of some of the activities which make up the project. These re-evaluated duration times are shown in Table 12.

Table 12 Table of activities with the revised duration times for network A

	Activity	Preceding activity	Duration (days)
Opening	A	–	3
	B	A	9
	C	A	*6 (7)
	D	B	*3 (5)
	E	B	*5 (4)
	F	C	3
	G	D	*3 (4)
	H	A, E	3
	J	F	7
	K	G, H, J	4

* Re-evaluated activity time (old activity time shown in brackets).

Re-evaluation has shown that:

- Activity C can be reduced from a duration time of 7 days to 6 days (i.e. the duration time of activity C can be crashed by 1 day).
- Activity D can be reduced from 5 days to 3 days (i.e. the duration time of activity D can be crashed by 2 days).
- Activity G can be reduced from 4 days to 3 days (i.e. the duration time of activity G can be crashed by 1 day).

However, vital resources which were used before crashing solely by activity E, are now being jointly used by activities C, D, E and G. As a result the duration time for activity E has increased from 4 days to 5 days. The changes in network A are shown in Figure 45 as network A1.

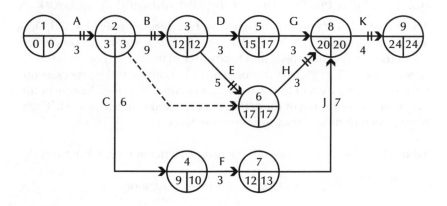

Figure 45   Network A1 showing the alterations in the critical path of network A

When comparing network A1, Figure 45, with network A, Figure 44, it can be seen that the critical path has altered from the old path of activities A, B, D, G and K (i.e. events 1, 2, 3, 5, 8 and 9) to the new critical path of activities A, B, E, H and K (i.e. events 1, 2, 3, 6, 8 and 9). This is because activities D and G are no longer critical:

- Activity G has 2 days spare. i.e. $(20 - 15) - 3 = 2$ days.
- Activity D has 2 days spare. i.e. $(17 - 12) - 3 = 2$ days.

The process of crashing has reduced the TPT from 25 days down to 24 days, thus resulting in a reduction of 1 day in the TPT. As a result, management now has to direct more of their attention to the new critical path shown in network A1, Figure 45.

It should be noted that it is not always beneficial to alter the direction of the critical path through a network because of the effect that this can have on other activities. In such a case the duration times of those activities which do not occur along the critical path should only be reduced to the extent that these same activities do not themselves become part of a critical path.

6.3   Caution when assigning the critical path

It is not always true that the critical path lies along the path of an activity where the earliest event time (EET) and the latest event time (LET) of the tail event of an activity are the same; and the EET and the LET of the head event of the activity are the same. This is shown in network B, Figure 46.

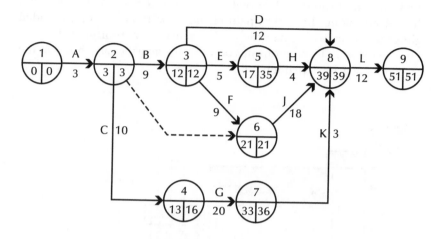

Figure 46   Network B

The following example of the need for caution when assigning the critical path concerns activity D of Network B.

- The EET for event 3 is 12 days.
- The LET for event 3 is 12 days.

and:

- The EET for event 8 is 39 days.
- The LET for event 8 is 39 days.

If the EET of 12 days for event 3 is subtracted from the LET of 39 days for event 8, the resulting time available to complete activity D is 27 days. However, activity D has a duration time of 12 days. Therefore, there are 15 days spare between the 27 days available and the 12 duration days required. This calculation is shown in tabulated form in Table 13.

Table 13   The calculation of the 'spare time' of activity D of network B

	LET of event 8	39 days
minus	EET of event 3	12 days
	Time available to complete activity D	**27 days**
minus	Duration time of activity D	12 days
	Spare time (float) after completing activity D 15 days	

6.4 The Gantt chart for network A

The Gantt chart shown as Figure 47 represents network A. The activities which occur along the critical path of the network are shown as shaded light grey activity bars. The grey shaded activity bars represent the non-critical activities. The relationships between the activities are shown by the succeeding activity dependency lines.

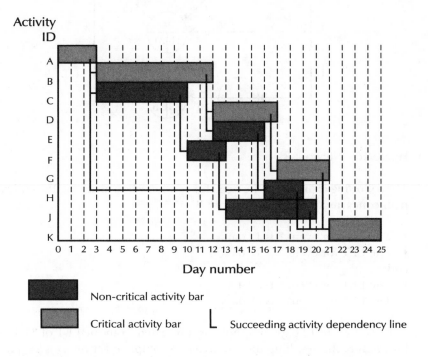

Figure 47   The Gantt chart for network A

A Gantt chart can be useful for analysing the relationships between activities. For example, the required use of a dummy activity to represent the relationship between activity A and activity H in network A, is avoided in the Gantt chart as the relationship is defined by the succeeding activity dependency line.

7 Float times

7.1 Introduction

An activity which possesses spare time can be completed over a longer period of time. This spare time is referred to as float or float time. Unless there is only one path through the network, all the paths in the network, with the nominal exclusion of the critical path, will have some sort of float.

Management may decide to share or remove a key resource which had been used to complete a particular activity which lies along a non-critical path (i.e. a path which contains float). As a result, the activity will take longer to complete. By reducing the float time of the activity (e.g. by allowing the activity to take longer to complete) the non-critical path may be lengthened. If the float time is further reduced a new critical path may be formed and, as a result, the old critical path could become non-critical.

In Figure 48, network A, path 3 (events 1, 2, 3, 6, 8 and 9), which is a non-critical path, includes activities E and H. Activities E and H can, between them, use up two days float without path 3 becoming critical.

Management can manoeuvre within the float of an activity, or a group of activities, to a limit which does not result in an alteration of the direction of the critical path. However, it should not be ruled out that management may intentionally alter the direction of the critical path.

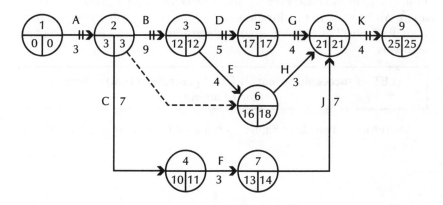

Figure 48 Network A with the forward pass and backward pass complete and the critical path defined

- Path 1 = activities A, B, D, G and K (events 1, 2, 3, 5, 8 and 9) = 25 days.
- Path 2 = activities A, C, F, J and K (events 1, 2, 4, 7, 8 and 9) = 24 days.
- Path 3 = activities A, B, E, H and K (events 1, 2, 3, 6, 8 and 9) = 23 days.

The types of float which most concern a network are total float, free float and independent float. The network shown in Figure 49 will be used to assist in the discussion of these types of float.

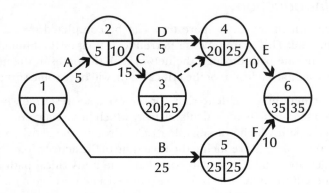

Figure 49 An AoA network containing total, free and independent float

7.2 Total float

Total float is the maximum amount of spare time possessed by an activity which can be used up by the activity without delaying the total project time (TPT). The total float possessed by an activity is measured when the earliest event time (EET) of the tail event of the activity and the latest event time (LET) of the head event of the activity are at their greatest distance apart. An increase in the duration time of the activity will reduce the total float available. The formula used to determine the total float time of an activity is:

> **(LET of succeeding event – EET of preceding event) – duration time of activity**

Therefore, activity D in Figure 49 has total float of 15 days; i.e. (25 – 5) – 5 = 15.

7.3   Free float

The free float available to an activity is the amount of float time which can be used up to complete the activity without affecting the EST of a succeeding activity (i.e. the activity and the succeeding activity both start at their EST). The formula used to calculate the free float of an activity is:

(EET of succeeding event – EET of preceding event) – duration time of activity

---

Therefore, activity D in Figure 49 has free float of 10 days; i.e. $(20 – 5) – 5 = 10$.

7.4   Independent float

Independent float is the amount of spare time possessed by an activity which it can use up without affecting the float of a preceding or succeeding activity. This will result in the time difference between the LET of the tail event of the activity and the EET of the head event of the activity being as small as possible. If a decision is made to reduce, or remove, a resource which is being used by a specific activity, it is possible to utilise the independent float of an activity without subsequently affecting the float of other activities.

Independent float does not occur often and where it does occur can often have a zero or negative value. The formula used to calculate the independent float of an activity is:

Minimum time available to complete activity 'X' – its duration time

---

NB: Minimum time available = EET of succeeding event – LET of preceding event

Therefore, activity D in Figure 49 has independent float of 5 days; i.e. $(20 – 10) – 5 = 5$.

A float time bar chart which illustrates the total, free and independent float of activity D in Figure 49, is shown as Figure 50.

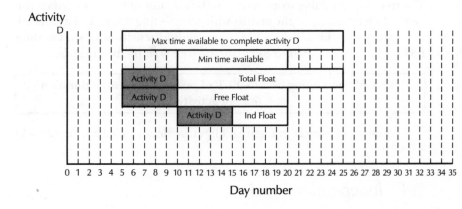

Figure 50 A float time bar chart of the total, free and independent float of activity D in Figure 49

A summary table of network A, which includes total, free and independent float times, is shown as Table 14. It should be noted that when calculating the float of an activity the relevant event times are used.

Table 14 A summary table including the total float, free float and independent float for the activities of network A

Activity	Duration (days)	Start EST	Start LST	Finish EFT	Finish LFT	Total float	Free float	Ind. float
A	3	0	0	3	3	0	0	0
B	9	3	3	12	12	0	0	0
C	7	3	4	10	11	1	0	0
D	5	12	12	17	17	0	0	0
E	4	12	14	16	18	2	0	0
F	3	10	11	13	14	1	0	-1
G	4	17	17	21	21	0	0	0
H	3	16	18	19	21	2	2	0
J	7	13	14	20	21	1	1	0
K	4	21	21	25	25	0	0	0

8 The Activity on Node (AoN) method

8.1 The Activity on Node method – an introduction

An alternative method, in comparison to the Activity on Arrow (AoA) method, of pictorially representing and analysing networks, is the Activity on Node (AoN) method. In the AoN method, the activities of a project are pictorially defined in a network as boxes (referred to as nodes). The relationships between the activities are defined by arrows (referred to as dependency arrows). A considerable advantage that the AoN method has over the AoA method is that it is quite often easier to define the relationships between the activities using the AoN method. This is because the AoN method does not require the use of dummy activities to maintain the logic of the network.

8.1.1 An activity node

An activity represents work which is performed as a part of the overall project and denotes a passage of time (e.g. *Wait for glue to set*) rather than only a 'physical' execution of work. Each activity is pictorially defined as a box which is referred to as a node. The information contained in the node refers to the activity which the node represents, an example of which is shown as Figure 51. Time flows from left-to-right as the AoN network progresses. As a result, a succeeding activity which is dependent upon the prior completion of a preceding activity, will be shown to the right of the node to which it is dependent upon.

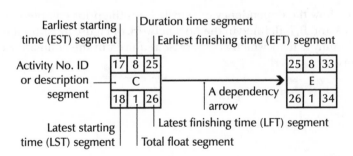

Figure 51   An AoN activity node

8.1.2 A dependency arrow

The relationships between the activities of a network are pictorially defined by the use of dependency arrows. An AoN network does not contain dummy activities and any dependency that one or more succeeding activities have on any preceding activities is defined by the dependency arrows. Various examples of AoN logic, in comparison to AoA logic, are shown in Figure 52 through to Figure 58.

8.2   Examples of Activity on Node logic

Activity	Precedes activity
A	C
B	C

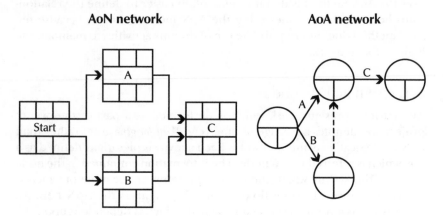

Figure 52   AoN network logic – at the start of a network (Example 1).

Note how the dependency of activity C on the prior completion of activities A and B, is defined in the AoN network of Figure 52 without the use of a dummy activity which is otherwise required in the comparative AoA network.

Activity	Precedes activity
A	C
B	D

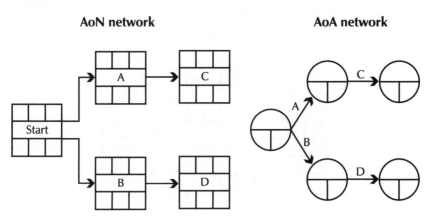

AoN network   **AoA network**

Figure 53   AoN network logic – at the start of a network (Example 2)

1   An AoN network does not contain any dummy activities.
2   Each activity in an AoN network is pictorially defined as a box which is referred to as a **node**.
3   The relationships between the activities of an AoN network are pictorially defined by the use of **dependency arrows**.

Activity	Precedes activity
E	F, G, H
F	H
G	H

AoN network

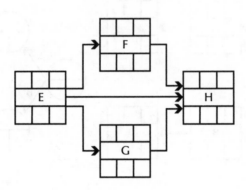

AoA network

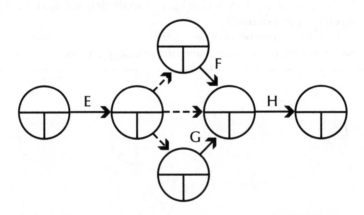

Figure 54   AoN network logic – dependency in a network (Example 1)

Note the use of three dependency arrows in the AoN network in Figure 54, which lead from activity E and then lead into activities F, G and H. In comparison, the AoA network requires the use of three dummy activities so as to maintain the logic of the network in accordance with the table of activities.

Activity	Precedes activity
G	J, M
H	K
J	L
K	M

AoN network

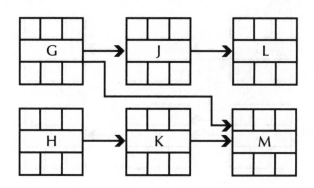

AoA network

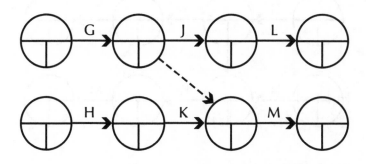

Figure 55 AoN network logic – dependency in a network (Example 2)

Activity	Precedes activity
G	J, K
H	K
J	L
K	M

AoN network

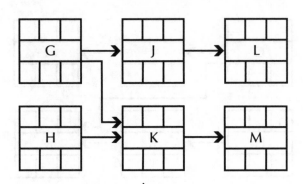

AoA network

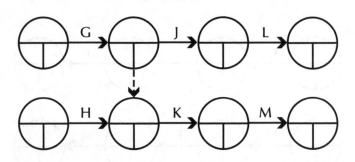

Figure 56 AoN network logic – dependency in a network (Example 3)

Activity	Precedes activity
L	N
M	P
N	–
P	–

– Denotes the finish of the network

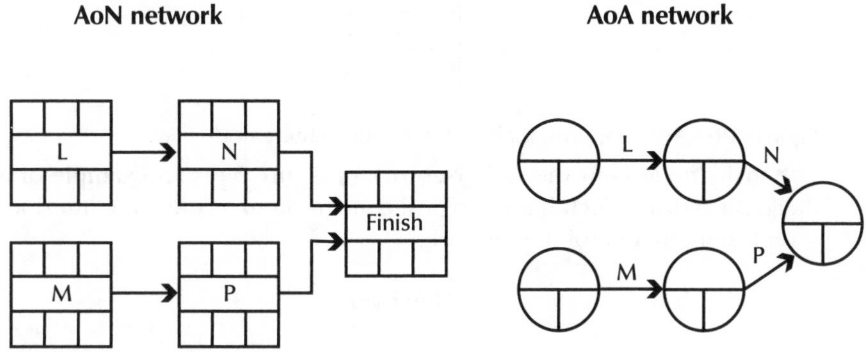

AoN network   **AoA network**

Figure 57   AoN network logic – at the finish of a network (Example 1)

Activity	Precedes activity
L	M
M	–

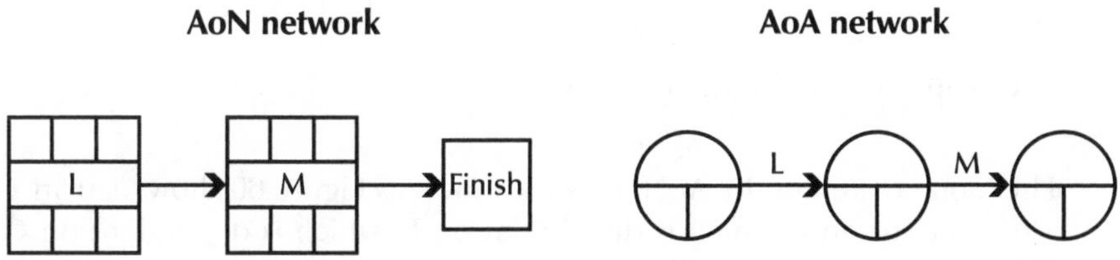

AoN network   **AoA network**

Figure 58   AoN network logic – at the finish of a network (Example 2)

AoN network

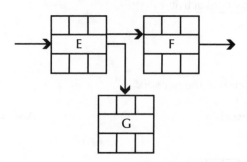

Figure 59   AoN network logic – a dangling activity node

Activity node G in the AoN Network of Figure 59 is an example of a dangling activity which has no logical conclusion to its outcome nor does it represent the end of the network.

AoN network

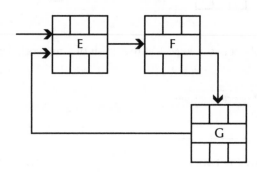

Figure 60   AoN network logic – looping

The loop created in the AoN network shown as Figure 60 shows activity G is dependent on F, which is dependent on E, which is dependent on G. This loop results in preceding activity E occurring after succeeding activity G.

8.3   The forward pass in an AoN network

The purpose of the forward pass is to determine the EST of each activity which will not affect the TPT or the logic of the network. Each EST is calculated while progressively moving from left-to-right across the network. The first node of the network is assigned as the start node and will have an EST of 0 days, that is unless the start of the project has been assigned a specific EST (e.g. 6 days). The EST of a succeeding activity is equal to the completion time of the preceding activity whose dependency arrow leads into the succeeding activity. When a succeeding activity has more than one dependency arrow leading into it, the EST of the succeeding activity is determined by the latest completion time out of the preceding activities whose dependency arrows lead into the activity. The EST of an activity is assigned to the EST segment of the relevant node and can be calculated using the following formula:

> **EST of activity 'X' = EST of preceding activity + its duration time**

The EFT of an activity (i.e. the earliest time an activity can finish without affecting the TPT or the logic of the network) is calculated by adding the duration time of the activity to the EST of the activity. The EFT of an activity is assigned to the EFT segment of the relevant node and is calculated using the following formula:

> **EFT of activity 'X' = EST of activity 'X' + its duration time**

The following example of calculating the EST and the EFT of an activity during the forward pass relates to Figure 61.

The EST of activity K is determined by the latest completion time out of the preceding activities whose dependency arrows lead into activity K. The calculation of the EST for activity K is as follows:

- Completion time of activity E = 25 + 8 = 33 days.
- Completion time of activity G = 33 + 6 = 39 days.
- Completion time of activity H = 38 + 2 = 40 days.

Therefore, the EST of activity K is 40 days and is assigned to the EST segment of the node for activity K.

The calculation of the EFT for activity K is as follows:

- EFT of activity K = 40 + 12 = 52 days.

The EFT of 52 days is assigned to the EFT segment of activity node K.

The EST of the finish node of the network is determined by the latest completion time out of the activities which lead into the finish node (i.e. activities K and L). Therefore, the EST of the finish node of the network is 52 days and is assigned to the EST segment of the finish node of the network. The EST and EFT of the finish of the network are the same because the finish of the network is instantaneous.

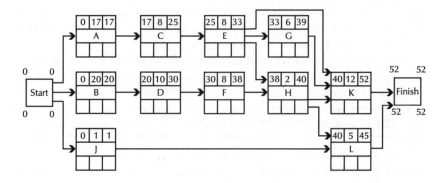

Figure 61 An AoN network showing the principle of the forward pass

8.4 The backward pass in an AoN network

The purpose of the backward pass is to determine the LST for each activity and to assist in the identification of the critical path. The LST of an activity is the latest time by which an activity can start without affecting the TPT or the logic of the network. The backward pass starts from the finish node of the network (which will nominally have an EST and a LST which are the same because the start and finish of the finish of the network is instantaneous) and is performed by calculating the LST for each activity while progressively moving from right-to-left across the network. The LST of an activity is calculated by subtracting the duration time of the activity from the LST of the succeeding activity. When an activity has more than one dependency arrow leading from it, the LST of the activity is calculated by subtracting the duration time of the activity from the LST of each of the succeeding activities so as to obtain the earliest LST. The LST of an activity is assigned to the LST segment of the relevant node and can be calculated using the following formula:

> **LST of activity 'X' = LST of succeeding activity – duration time of activity 'X'**

The LFT of an activity is determined by adding the duration time of the activity to the LST of the activity. The LFT of an activity is the latest time by which an activity can finish without affecting the TPT or the logic of the network and is assigned to the LFT segment of the relevant node. The LFT of an activity can be calculated using the following formula:

> **LFT of activity 'X' = LST of activity 'X' + its duration time**

The following example of calculating the LST and the LFT of an activity during the backward pass relates to activity E of Figure 62.

The LST of activity E is determined by the earliest LST value which is obtained by subtracting the duration time of activity E from the LST of each of the activities which succeed activity E. The calculation of the LST for activity E is as follows:

- LST of activity K – duration time of E = 40 – 8 = 32 days.
- LST of activity H – duration time of E = 38 – 8 = 30 days.
- LST of activity G – duration time of E = 34 – 8 = 26 days.

Therefore, the LST of activity E is 26 days and is assigned to the LST segment of the node for activity K.

The calculation of the LFT for activity E is as follows:

- LFT of activity E = 26 + 8 = 34 days.

The LFT of 34 days is assigned to the LFT segment of activity node E.

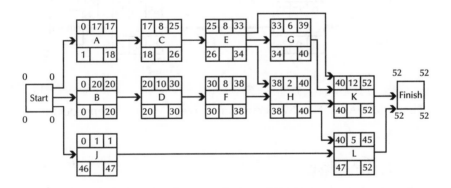

Figure 62   An AoN network showing the principle of the backward pass

8.5   Float time in an AoN network

An activity which possesses spare time can be completed over a longer period of time. This spare time is referred to as float or float time. Unless there is only one path through the network, all the paths in the network, with the nominal exclusion of the critical path, will have some sort of float.

71

8.5.1 Total float

Total float is the amount of spare time possessed by the activity which can be used up by the activity without affecting the total project time (TPT). The activity node in an AoN network has provision for the inclusion of the total float value possessed by an activity, which can be determined using the following formula:

> **Total float of activity 'X' = LST of activity 'X' – EST of activity 'X'**

Activity D in Figure 63 has total float of 15 days (i.e. 20 – 5 = 15).

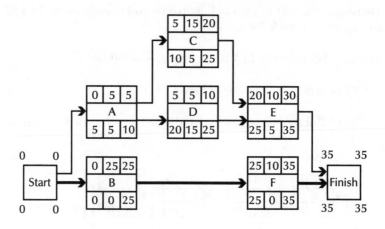

Figure 63   An AoN network containing total, free and independent float

8.5.2 Free float

The free float of an activity is the amount of spare time possessed by an activity which can be used up by the activity without affecting the EST of any succeeding activity or the TPT. If the activity under consideration finishes at a head event from which more than one activity starts, then the free float of the activity under consideration will be determined by the earliest EST out of the succeeding activities. The free float of an activity can be determined by the use of the following formula:

Free float of = the LFT of activity 'X' which will not affect	−	EFT of
activity 'X' the float in a succeeding activity		activity 'X'

Activity D in Figure 63 has free float of 10 days (i.e. 20 − 10 = 10). This is because the LFT of activity D which will not affect the float in activity E is 20 days (20 days is the EST of activity E). The EFT of activity D (i.e. 10 days) is subtracted to give a free float value of 10 days for activity D.

8.5.3   Independent float

Independent float is the amount of spare time possessed by an activity which, if used up, will not affect the float time in a preceding or succeeding activity. Therefore, the time between the EST of the activity which succeeds the activity under consideration, and the LFT of the activity which precedes the activity under consideration, will be as small as possible. The duration time of the activity under consideration is then subtracted from relevant succeeding EST − preceding LFT value to give the independent float of the activity under consideration.

Where the activity under consideration precedes more than one activity, the earliest EST out of the succeeding activities is used in the calculation of the independent float time of the activity under consideration. Where the activity under consideration succeeds more than one activity, the latest LFT of any of the preceding activities is used in the independent float calculation of the activity under consideration.

Independent float does not often occur and when it does it normally has a zero or negative value. The independent float of an activity can be determined by the use of the following formula:

Ind float of = the LFT of activity	−	the EST of activity	−	duration
activity 'X' 'X' which will not affect the float of a succeeding activity		'X' which will not affect the float of a preceding activity		time of activity 'X'

Activity D in Figure 63 has independent float of 5 days i.e. (20 − 10) − 5 = 5. The 20 days in the calculation refers to the LFT of activity D (which is determined by the EST of activity E); the 10 days refers to the EST activity D because 10 days is the LFT of activity A. The 5 days which is subtracted refers to the duration time of activity D.

8.6   Identifying the critical path in an AoN network

The critical path in an AoN network occurs along the path of activities which has the most minimal float (this will result in the EST and the LST of an activity being the same; and the EFT and the LFT of the activity being the same). To define the critical path on the network, the dependency arrows of the activities which occur along the critical path are drawn thicker than the other dependency arrows occurring along the non-critical path(s) in the network. The critical path for the network shown as Figure 64 occurs through activity nodes B, D, F, H and K.

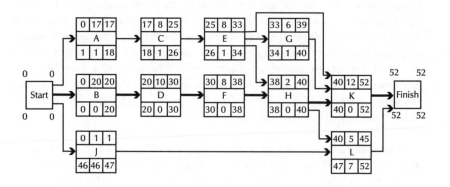

Figure 64   The critical path identified in an AoN network

8.7 A worked example of the forward pass, the backward pass and identification of the critical path in an AoN network – Network A

Table 15 lists the activities and duration times for network A, which is shown as Figure 65.

Table 15 The table of activities for network A

	Activity	Preceding activity	Duration*
Opening	A	–	3
	B	A	9
	C	A	7
	D	B	5
	E	B	4
	F	C	3
	G	D	4
	H	A, E	3
	J	F	7
Closing	K	G, H, J	4

* Duration time in days.

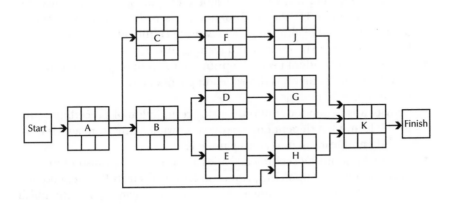

Figure 65 Network A

8.7.1   The drawing of network A (AoN method)

- There are no preceding activities before activity A. One dependency arrow is shown leading from the start node of the network and then leading into an activity node which represents activity A.
- There are three activities dependent upon the prior completion of activity A (i.e. activities B, C and H). Therefore, three dependency arrows are shown leading from activity A. One arrow leads into activity node B; another arrow leads into activity node C; and the other arrow will lead into activity node H.
- Activity D is dependent upon the prior completion of preceding activity B. Once activity B has finished, activity D can start. A dependency arrow is shown leading from activity node B and leading into activity node D.
- Activity E is also dependent upon the prior completion of preceding activity B. Once activity B has finished, activity E can start. A dependency arrow is shown leading from activity node B and leading into activity node E.
- Activity F is dependent upon the prior completion of preceding activity C. A dependency arrow is shown leading from activity node C and leading into activity node F.
- Activity G is dependent upon the prior completion of preceding activity D. A dependency arrow is shown leading from activity node D and leading into activity node G.
- Activity H is dependent upon the prior completion of preceding activity E and preceding activity A. Two dependency arrows are shown leading into activity node H: one dependency arrow is shown leading from activity node E and leading into activity node H; the other arrow is shown leading from activity node A and leading into activity node H.
- Activity J is dependent upon the prior completion of preceding activity F. A dependency arrow is shown leading from activity node F and leading into activity node J.
- Activity K is dependent upon the prior completion of preceding activities G, H and J. A dependency arrow is shown leading from activities G, H and J and leading into activity node K.
- Activity K has no succeeding activities. As a result, the finish of the network is dependent upon the prior completion of activity K. A dependency arrow is shown leading from activity K and then leading into the finish node of the network.

There are 10 activity nodes to represent the 10 activities of network A

8.7.2 The forward pass for network A (AoN method)

Calculations involved in the forward pass make use of the following formulae:

EST of activity 'X' = EST of preceding activity + its duration time

---

EFT of activity 'X' = EST of activity 'X' + its duration time

---

- Unless clearly stated otherwise, the EST of the start node of the network will be 0 days. Because the start and finish of the start of the network is instantaneous the EFT will also be 0 days. The EST and the EFT are assigned to the start node.
- The EST of activity A is 0 days. This is because activity A starts at the start of the network. The EST of 0 days is assigned to the EST segment of activity A. The EFT for activity A is 3 days (0 + 3 = 3) and is assigned to the EFT segment of activity A.
- Activity B has only one dependency arrow leading into it (i.e. the arrow from activity A). The EST of activity B is 3 days (0 + 3 = 3) and is assigned to the EST segment of activity B. The EFT for activity B is 12 days (3 + 9 = 12) and is assigned to the EFT segment of activity B.
- Activity C has only one dependency arrow leading into it (i.e. the arrow from activity A). The EST of activity C is 3 days (0 + 3 = 3) and is assigned to the EST segment of activity C. The EFT for activity C is 10 days (3 + 7 = 10) and is assigned to the EFT segment of activity C.
- Activity D has only one dependency arrow leading into it (i.e. the arrow from activity B). The EST of activity D is 12 days (3 + 9 = 12) and is assigned to the EST segment of activity D. The EFT for activity D is 17 days (12 + 5 = 17) and is assigned to the EFT segment of activity D.
- Activity E has only one dependency arrow leading into it (i.e. the arrow from activity B). Therefore, the EST of activity E is 12 days (3 + 9 = 12) and is assigned to the EST segment of activity E. The EFT for activity E is 16 days (12 + 4 = 16) and is assigned to the EFT segment of activity E.
- Activity F has only one dependency arrow leading into it (i.e. the arrow from activity C). The EST of activity F is 10 days (3 + 7 = 10) and is assigned to the EST segment of activity F. The EFT for activity F is 13 days (10 + 3 = 13) and is assigned to the EFT segment of activity F.
- Activity G has only one dependency arrow leading into it (i.e. the arrow from activity D). The EST of activity G is 17 days (12 + 5 = 17) and is assigned to the EST segment of activity G. The EFT for activity G is 21 days (17 + 4 = 21) and is assigned to the EFT segment of activity G.
- Activity H has two dependency arrows leading into it (i.e. the arrows from activities A and E). The EST of activity H is determined by the

preceding activity with the latest completion time. The EST for activity H is calculated as follows:
- EST of activity A + its duration time = 3 days $(0 + 3 = 3)$.
- EST of activity E + its duration time = 16 days $(12 + 4 = 16)$.

The EST of activity H is 16 days and is assigned to the EST segment of activity H. The EFT for activity H is 19 days $(16 + 3 = 19)$ and is assigned to the EFT segment of activity H.

- Activity J has only one dependency arrow leading into it (i.e. the arrow from activity F). The EST of activity J is 13 days $(10 + 3 = 13)$ and is assigned to the EST segment of activity J. The EFT for activity J is 20 days $(13 + 7 = 20)$ and is assigned to the EFT segment of activity J.

- Activity K has three dependency arrows leading into it (i.e. the arrows from activities G, H and J). The EST of activity K is determined by the preceding activity with the latest completion time. The EST for activity K is calculated as follows:
- EST of activity G + its duration time = 21 days $(17 + 4 = 21)$.
- EST of activity H + its duration time = 19 days $(16 + 3 = 19)$.
- EST of activity J + its duration time = 20 days $(13 + 7 = 20)$.

The EST of activity K is 21 days and is assigned to the EST segment of activity K. The EFT for activity K is 25 days $(21 + 4 = 25)$ and is assigned to the EFT segment of activity K.

- Because activity K is the last activity in the project, the EST of the finish node of the network is determined as follows:
- Completion time of activity K = 25 days $(21 + 4 = 25)$.

The EST of the finish node of the network is 25 days and is assigned to the finish node. The EFT, LST and LFT of the finish node will be the same as the EST because the start and finish of the finish of the network is instantaneous.

The minimum amount of time required to complete the project is 25 days. Therefore, the TPT for Network A is 25 days.

The completed forward pass for Network A is shown as Figure 66.

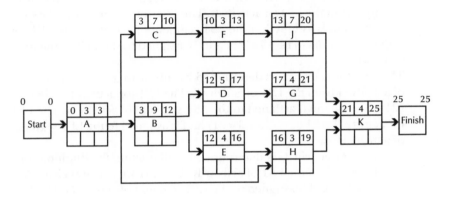

Figure 66   Network A with the forward pass completed

---

1   The EST of a succeeding activity is equal to the completion time of the preceding activity whose dependency arrow leads into the succeeding activity (completion time = EST of preceding activity + its duration time).

2   The EST of a succeeding activity, which has more than one dependency arrow leading into it, is determined by the latest completion time out of the preceding activities whose dependency arrows lead into the succeeding activity.

3   The EFT of an activity is determined by the EST of the activity + its duration time.

8.7.3   The backward pass for network A (AoN method)

Calculations involved in the backward pass make use of the following formulae:

LST of activity 'X' = LST of succeeding activity – duration time of activity 'X'

LFT of activity 'X' = LST of activity 'X' + its duration time

---

• The LST for activity K is determined by subtracting the duration time of activity K from the LST of the finish node (25 – 4 = 21). The LST of 21 days is assigned to the LST segment of activity K. The LFT for activity K is 25 days (21 + 4 = 25).

79

- The LST for activity J is determined by subtracting the duration time of activity J from the LST of activity K. The LST for activity J is 14 days (21 − 7 = 14) and is assigned to the LST segment of activity J. The LFT for activity J is 21 days (14 + 7 = 21) and is assigned to the LFT segment of activity J.
- The LST for activity H is determined by subtracting the duration time of activity H from the LST of activity K. The LST for activity H is 18 days (21 − 3 = 18) and is assigned to the LST segment of activity H. The LFT for activity H is 21 days (18 + 3 = 21) and is assigned to the LFT segment of activity H.
- The LST for activity G is determined by subtracting the duration time of activity G from the LST of activity K. The LST for activity G is 17 days (21 − 4 = 17) and is assigned to the LST segment of activity G. The LFT for activity G is 21 days (17 + 4 = 21) and is assigned to the LFT segment of activity G.
- The LST for activity F is determined by subtracting the duration time of activity F from the LST of activity J. The LST for activity F is 11 days (14 − 3 = 11) and is assigned to the LST segment of activity F. The LFT for activity F is 14 days (11 + 3 = 14) and is assigned to the LFT segment of activity F.
- The LST for activity E is determined by subtracting the duration time of activity E from the LST of activity H. The LST for activity E is 14 days (18 − 4 = 14) and is assigned to the LST segment of activity E. The LFT for activity E is 18 days (14 + 4 = 18) and is assigned to the LFT segment of activity E.
- The LST for activity D is determined by subtracting the duration time of activity D from the LST of activity G. The LST for activity D is 12 days (17 − 5 = 12) and is assigned to the LST segment of activity D. The LFT for activity D is 17 days (12 + 5 = 17) and is assigned to the LFT segment of activity D.
- The LST for activity C is determined by subtracting the duration time of activity C from the LST of activity F. The LST for activity C is 4 days (11 − 7 = 4) and is assigned to the LST segment of activity C. The LFT for activity C is 11 days (4 + 7 = 11) and is assigned to the LFT segment of activity C.
- The LST for activity B is determined by the earliest time obtained from subtracting the duration time of activity B from the LST of each of the activities which succeed activity B (i.e. activities D and E). The LST for activity B is calculated as follows:
  - LST of activity E − duration time of activity B = 5 days (14 − 9 = 5).
  - LST of activity D − duration time of activity B = 3 days (12 − 9 = 3).
  The LST of activity B is 3 days and is assigned to the LST segment of activity B. The LFT for activity B is 12 days (3 + 9 = 12) and is assigned to the LFT segment of activity B.

- The LST for activity A is determined by the earliest time obtained from subtracting the duration time of activity A from the LST of each of the activities which succeed activity A (i.e. activities B, C and H). The LST for activity A is calculated as follows:
  - LST of activity H – duration time of activity A = 15 days (18 – 3 = 15).
  - LST of activity C – duration time of activity A = 1 day (4 – 3 = 1).
  - LST of activity B – duration time of activity A = 0 days (3 – 3 = 0).

  The LST of activity A is 0 days and is assigned to the LST segment of activity A. The LFT for activity A is 3 days (0 + 3 = 3) and is assigned to the LFT segment of activity A.
- Because activity A is the only activity to start at the beginning of the network, the LST of activity A represents the LST of the start of the network. The LST of 0 days is assigned to the start node of the network. Because the EST, EFT and LST of the start of the network is 0 days, the LFT of the start node of the network is also 0 days. This is because the start and the finish of the start of the network is instantaneous. The LFT is assigned to the start node of the network.

The completed backward pass for network A is shown as Figure 67.

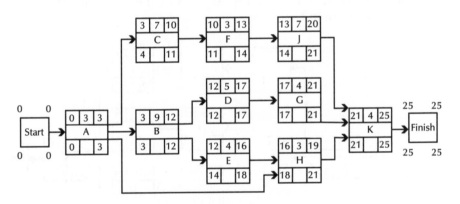

Figure 67 Network A with the backward pass completed

8.7.4 The total, free and independent float possessed by the activities in network A

A summary table of network A, which includes total, free and independent float times, is shown as Table 16. It should be noted that when calculating the float of an activity the relevant times are used.

Table 16 A summary table of network A

Activity	Duration (days)	Start EST	LST	Finish EFT	LFT	Total Float	Free Float	Ind Float
A	3	0	0	3	3	0	0	0
B	9	3	3	12	12	0	0	0
C	7	3	4	10	11	1	0	0
D	5	12	12	17	17	0	0	0
E	4	12	14	16	18	2	0	0
F	3	10	11	13	14	1	0	-1
G	4	17	17	21	21	0	0	0
H	3	16	18	19	21	2	2	0
J	7	13	14	20	21	1	1	0
K	4	21	21	25	25	0	0	0

8.7.5 The critical path in network A (AoN method)

The critical path for network A occurs along the path of activities which has minimal float. Therefore the critical path for network A occurs through activity nodes A, B, D, G and K, which is defined by bold dependency arrows, as shown in Figure 68.

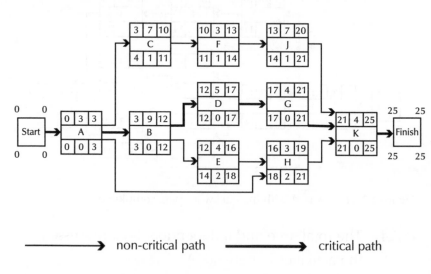

Figure 68 Network A with the critical path defined

9 Network C – A worked example using AoA method without dummy activities; and the AoN method

9.1 Example 2 – Network C (AoA method)

Table 17 lists the activities and duration times for network C, which is shown as Figure 69.

Table 17 The table of activities for network C

Activity	Precedes activity	Duration*
A	C	4
B	D, E	12
C	H	20
D	F	2
E	G	6
F	J	12
G	K	6
H	–	17
J	–	16
K	–	15

* Duration time in days.

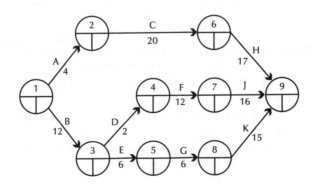

Figure 69 Network C

9.1.1   The drawing of network C (AoA method)

- There are no preceding activities before activities A and B. Activities A and B represent the start of the network and are shown starting from event 1.
- Activity C is dependent upon the prior completion of activity A which finishes at event 2. Once activity A has finished at event 2, activity C can start from event 2.
- Activities D and E are dependent upon the prior completion of activity B. As a result, activities D and E can start from event 3 once activity B has finished at event 3.
- Activity F is dependent upon the prior completion of preceding activity D. Once activity D has finished at event 4, activity F can start from event 4.
- Activity G is dependent upon the prior completion of preceding activity E. Once activity E has finished at event 5, activity G can start from event 5.
- Activity H is dependent upon the prior completion of preceding activity C. Once activity C has finished at event 6, activity H can start from event 6.
- Activity J is dependent upon the prior completion of preceding activity F. Once activity F has finished at event 7, activity J can start from event 7.
- Activity K is dependent upon the prior completion of preceding activity G. Once activity G has finished at event 8, activity K can start from event 8.
- The completion of activities H, J and K at event 9 represents the finish of the network.

Network C has 10 activities and 9 events

9.1.2   The forward pass for network C (AoA method)

Calculations involved in the forward pass make use of the following formula:

EST of activity 'X' = EST of preceding activity + its duration time

---

- Event 1 has an EET of 0 days which is assigned to the event. Activities A and B start at day 0.
- Event 2 has an EET of 4 days (0 + 4 = 4) which is assigned to the event. Activity C can start at day 4.
- Event 3 has an EET of 12 days (0 + 12 = 12) which is assigned to the event. Activities D and E can start at day 12.

- Event 4 has an EET of 14 days (12 + 2 = 14) which is assigned to the event. Activity F can start at day 14.
- Event 5 has an EET of 18 days (12 + 6 = 18) which is assigned to the event. Activity G can start at day 18.
- Event 6 has an EET of 24 days (4 + 20 = 24) which is assigned to the event. Activity H can start at day 24.
- Event 7 has an EET of 26 days (14 + 12 = 26) which is assigned to the event. Activity J can start at day 26.
- Event 8 has an EET of 24 days (18 + 6 = 24) which is assigned to the event. Activity K can start at day 24.
- Event 9 has three activities finishing at it. The EET of event 9 is determined by the latest EFT of the activities which lead into this event. The calculation for event 9 is as follows:
  - EFT of activity H = 41 days (24 + 17 = 41).
  - EFT of activity J = 42 days (26 + 16 = 42).
  - EFT of activity K = 39 days (24 + 15 = 39).

  The EET for event 9 is 42 days because 42 days is the latest EFT out of all the activities which lead into event 9. The EET for event 9 is assigned to the event. Event 9 represents the finish event of Network C.

> **The minimum amount of time required to complete the project is 42 days. Therefore, the TPT for network C is 42 days.**

The completed forward pass for Network C is shown as Figure 70.

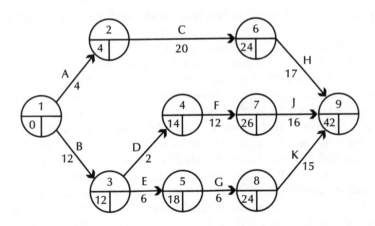

Figure 70 Network C with the forward pass completed

The EET calculations for network C, Figure 70, are shown in tabulated form in Table 18.

Table 18   The EET calculations for network C

Event	Calculations	EET (days)
1	0 + 0 =	0
2	0 + 4 =	4
3	0 + 12 =	12
4	12 + 2 =	14
5	12 + 6 =	18
6	4 + 20 =	24
7	14 + 12 =	26
8	18 + 6 =	24
9	26 + 16 =	42

The backward pass for network C is as follows:

9.1.3   The backward pass for network C (AoA method)

Calculations involved in the backward pass make use of the following formula:

LST of activity 'X' = LFT of activity 'X' – its duration time

---

- If the TPT of 42 days is to be observed the LET for event 9 will be 42 days.
- Event 8 has an LET of 27 days (42 – 15 = 27) which is assigned to the event. Activity G must finish by day 27 if activity K is to start by its LST.
- Event 7 has an LET of 26 days (42 – 16 = 26) which is assigned to the event. Activity F must finish by day 26 if activity J is to start by its LST.
- Event 6 has an LET of 25 days (42 – 17 = 25) which is assigned to the event. Activity C must finish by day 25 if activity H is to start by its LST.
- Event 5 has an LET of 21 days (27 – 6 = 21) which is assigned to the event. Activity E must finish by day 21 if activity G is to start by its LST.
- Event 4 has an LET of 14 days (26 – 12 = 14) which is assigned to the event. Activity D must finish by day 14 if activity F is to start by its LST.
- Event 3 has two activities starting from it. The LET of event 3 is determined by the earliest LST of the activities that start from event 3. The calculation for the LET of event 3 is as follows:
  - LST of activity E = 15 days (21 – 6 = 15).
  - LST of activity D = 12 days (14 – 2 = 12).
  The LET for event 3 is 12 days which is assigned to the event. Activity B must finish by day 12 if activity D is to start by its LST.

- Event 2 has an LET of 5 days $(25 - 20 = 5)$ which is assigned to the event. Activity A must finish by day 5 if activity C is to start by its LST.
- Event 1 has two activities starting from it. The LET of event 1 is determined by the earliest LST of the activities which start from event 1. The calculation for the LET of event 1 is as follows:
  - LST of activity B = 0 days $(12 - 12 = 0)$.
  - LST of activity A = 1 day $(5 - 4 = 1)$.
  The LET for event 1 is 0 days which is assigned to the event.

The completed backward pass for network C is shown as Figure 71.

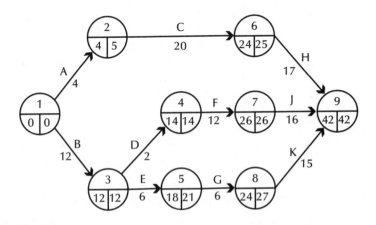

Figure 71   Network C with the backward pass completed

The LET calculations for network C in Figure 71 are shown in tabulated form in Table 19.

Table 19   The LET calculations for network C

Event	Calculations	LET (days)
8	42 – 15 =	27
7	42 – 16 =	26
6	42 – 17 =	25
5	27 – 6 =	21
4	26 – 12 =	14
3	14 – 2 =	12
2	25 – 20 =	5
1	12 – 12 =	0

9.1.4 The total, free and independent float possessed by the activities of network C

A summary table of network C, which includes total, free and independent float times, is shown as Table 20. It should be noted that when calculating the float of an activity the relevant event times are used.

Table 20   A summary table of network C

Activity	Duration (days)	Start EST	Start LST	Finish EFT	Finish LFT	Total Float	Free Float	Ind. Float
A	4	0	1	4	5	1	0	0
B	12	0	0	12	12	0	0	0
C	20	4	5	24	25	1	0	-1
D	2	12	12	14	14	0	0	0
E	6	12	15	18	21	3	0	0
F	12	14	14	26	26	0	0	0
G	6	18	21	24	27	3	0	-3
H	17	24	25	41	42	1	1	0
J	16	26	26	42	42	0	0	0
K	15	24	27	39	42	3	3	0

9.1.5 The critical path in network C (AoA method)

The critical path for network C occurs along the path of activities which has minimal float. Therefore, the critical path for network C occurs through activities B, D, F and J (i.e. events 1, 3, 4, 7 and 9). Network C is shown completed as Figure 72.

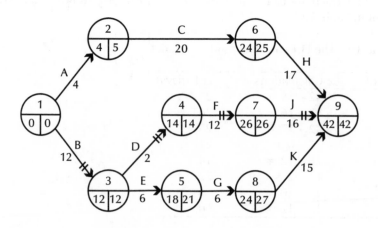

Figure 72   Network C with the critical path defined

9.2 Example 2 – Network C (AoN method)

Table 21 lists the activities and duration times for network C, which is shown as Figure 73.

Table 21 The table of activities for network C

Activity	Precedes activity	Duration*
A	C	4
B	D, E	12
C	H	20
D	F	2
E	G	6
F	J	12
G	K	6
H	–	17
J	–	16
K	–	15

* Duration time in days.

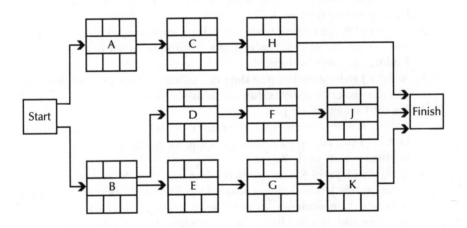

Figure 73 Network C

9.2.1   The drawing of network C (AoN method)

- There are no preceding activities before activities A and B. Two dependency arrows are shown leading from the start node of the network. One dependency arrow leads into an activity node which represents activity A; the other arrow leads into an activity node which represents activity B.
- Two activities are dependent upon the prior completion of activity B (i.e. activities D and E). Therefore, two activity nodes are shown to the right of activity B. One of these activity nodes represents activity D; the other node represents activity E. Two dependency arrows are shown leading from activity B. One arrow leads into activity node D; the other arrow leads into activity node E.
- Activity C is dependent upon the prior completion of activity A. A dependency arrow is shown leading from activity node A and leading into activity node C.
- Activity F is dependent upon the prior completion of preceding activity D. Once activity D has finished, activity F can start. A dependency arrow is shown leading from activity node D and leading into activity node F.
- Activity G is dependent upon the prior completion of preceding activity E. A dependency arrow is shown leading from activity node E and leading into activity node G.
- Activity H is dependent upon the prior completion of preceding activity C. A dependency arrow is shown leading from activity node C and leading into activity node H.
- Activity J is dependent upon the prior completion of preceding activity F. A dependency arrow is shown leading from activity node F and leading into activity node J.
- Activity K is dependent upon the prior completion of preceding activity G. A dependency arrow is shown leading from activity node G and leading into activity node K.
- Activities H, J and K have no succeeding activities. As a result, the finish of the network is dependent upon the prior completion of these three activities. A dependency arrow is shown leading from each of the three activities and then leading into the finish node of the network.

There are 10 activity nodes to represent the 10 activities of network C

9.2.2   The forward pass for network C (AoN method)

Calculations involved in the forward pass make use of the following formulae:

> **EST of activity 'X' = EST of preceding activity + its duration time**

> **EFT of activity 'X' = EST of activity 'X' + its duration time**

- Unless clearly stated otherwise, the EST of the start node of the network will be 0 days. Because the start and finish of the start of the network is instantaneous the EFT will also be 0 days. The EST and the EFT are assigned to the start node.
- The EST of activity A is 0 days. This is because activity A starts at the start of the network. The EST of 0 days is assigned to the EST segment of activity A. The EFT for activity A is 4 days $(0 + 4 = 4)$ and is assigned to the EFT segment of activity A.
- The EST of activity B is 0 days. This is because activity B starts at the start of the network. The EST of 0 days is assigned to the EST segment of activity B. The EFT for activity B is 12 days $(0 + 12 = 12)$ and is assigned to the EFT segment of activity B.
- Activity C has only one dependency arrow leading into it (i.e. the arrow from activity A). The EST of activity C is 4 days $(0 + 4 = 4)$ and is assigned to the EST segment of activity C. The EFT for activity C is 24 days $(4 + 20 = 24)$ and is assigned to the EFT segment of activity C.
- Activity D has only one dependency arrow leading into it (i.e. the arrow from activity B). The EST of activity D is 12 days $(0 + 12 = 12)$ and is assigned to the EST segment of activity D. The EFT for activity D is 14 days $(12 + 2 = 14)$ and is assigned to the EFT segment of activity D.
- Activity E has only one dependency arrow leading into it (i.e. the arrow from activity B). The EST of activity E is 12 days $(0 + 12 = 12)$ and is assigned to the EST segment of activity E. The EFT for activity E is 18 days $(12 + 6 = 18)$ and is assigned to the EFT segment of activity E.
- Activity F has only one dependency arrow leading into it (i.e. the arrow from activity D). The EST of activity F is 14 days $(12 + 2 = 14)$ and is assigned to the EST segment of activity F. The EFT for activity F is 26 days $(14 + 12 = 26)$ and is assigned to the EFT segment of activity F.
- Activity G has only one dependency arrow leading into it (i.e. the arrow from activity E). The EST of activity G is 18 days $(12 + 6 = 18)$ and is assigned to the EST segment of activity G. The EFT for activity G is 24 days $(18 + 6 = 24)$ and is assigned to the EFT segment of activity G.
- Activity H has only one dependency arrow leading into it (i.e. the arrow from activity C). The EST of activity H is 24 days $(4 + 20 = 24)$ and is assigned to the EST segment of activity H. The EFT for activity H is 41 days $(24 + 17 = 41)$ and is assigned to the EFT segment of activity H.

- Activity J has only one dependency arrow leading into it (i.e. the arrow from activity F). The EST of activity J is 26 days (14 + 12 = 26) and is assigned to the EST segment of activity J. The EFT for activity J is 42 days (26 + 16 = 42) and is assigned to the EFT segment of activity J.
- Activity K has only one dependency arrow leading into it (i.e. the arrow from activity G). The EST of activity G is 24 days (18 + 6 = 24) and is assigned to the EST segment of activity K. The EFT for activity K is 39 days (24 + 15 = 39) and is assigned to the EFT segment of activity K.
- The finish node of the network has three dependency arrows leading into it (i.e. the arrows from activities H, J and K). The EST of the finish node is determined by the preceding activity with the latest completion time. The EST for the finish node is calculated as follows:
  - EST of activity H + its duration time = 41 days (24 + 17 = 41).
  - EST of activity J + its duration time = 42 days (26 + 16 = 42).
  - EST of activity K + its duration time = 39 days (24 + 15 = 39).

The EST of the finish node of the network is 42 days and is assigned to the finish node. The EFT, LST and LFT of the finish node will be the same as the EST because the start and finish of the finish of the network is instantaneous.

The minimum amount of time required to complete the project is 42 days. Therefore, the TPT for network C is 42 days.

Network C is shown with the forward pass completed as Figure 74.

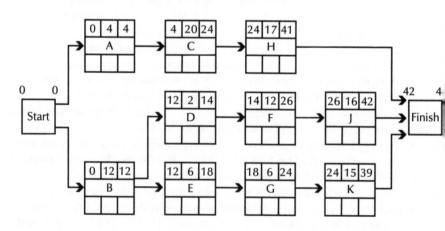

Figure 74 Network C with the forward pass completed

9.2.3 The backward pass for network C (AoN method)

Calculations involved in the backward pass make use of the following formulae:

> **LST of activity 'X' = LST of succeeding activity – duration
> time of activity 'X'**

> **LFT of activity 'X' = LST of activity 'X' + its duration time**

- The LST for activity K is determined by subtracting the duration time of activity K from the LST of the finish node (42 – 15 = 27). The LST of 27 days is assigned to the LST segment of activity K. The LFT for activity K is 42 days (27 + 15 = 42) and is assigned to the LFT segment of activity K.
- The LST for activity J is determined by subtracting the duration time of activity J from the LST of the finish node (42 – 16 = 26). The LST of 26 days is assigned to the LST segment of activity J. The LFT for activity J is 42 days (26 + 16 = 42) and is assigned to the LFT segment of activity J.
- The LST for activity H is determined by subtracting the duration time of activity H from the LST of the finish node (42 – 17 = 25). The LST of 25 days is assigned to the LST segment of activity H. The LFT for activity H is 42 days (25 + 17 = 42) and is assigned to the LFT segment of activity H.
- The LST for activity G is determined by subtracting the duration time of activity G from the LST of activity K. The LST for activity G is 21 days (27 – 6 = 21) and is assigned to the LST segment of activity G. The LFT for activity G is 27 days (21 + 6 = 27) and is assigned to the LFT segment of activity G.
- The LST for activity F is determined by subtracting the duration time of activity F from the LST of activity J. The LST for activity F is 14 days (26 – 12 = 14) and is assigned to the LST segment of activity F. The LFT for activity F is 26 days (14 + 12 = 26) and is assigned to the LFT segment of activity F.
- The LST for activity E is determined by subtracting the duration time of activity E from the LST of activity G. The LST for activity E is 15 days (21 – 6 = 15) and is assigned to the LST segment of activity E. The LFT for activity E is 21 days (15 + 6 = 21) and is assigned to the LFT segment of activity E.
- The LST for activity D is determined by subtracting the duration time of activity D from the LST of activity F. The LST for activity D is 12 days (14 – 2 = 12) and is assigned to the LST segment of activity D. The LFT

for activity D is 14 days (12 + 2 = 14) and is assigned to the LFT segment of activity D.

- The LST for activity C is determined by subtracting the duration time of activity C from the LST of activity H. The LST for activity C is 5 days (25 – 20 = 5) and is assigned to the LST segment of activity C. The LFT for activity C is 25 days (5 + 20 = 25) and is assigned to the LFT segment of activity C.

- The LST for activity B is determined by the smallest value obtained from subtracting the duration time of activity B from the LST of each activity which succeeds activity B (i.e. activities D and E). The LST for activity B is calculated as follows:
  - LST of activity E – duration time of activity B = 3 days (15 – 12 = 3).
  - LST of activity D – duration time of activity B = 0 days (12 – 12 = 0).
  The LST of activity B is 0 days and is assigned to the LST segment of activity B. The LFT for activity B is 12 days (0 + 12 = 12) and is assigned to the LFT segment of activity B.

- The LST for activity A is determined by subtracting the duration time of activity A from the LST of activity C. The LST for activity A is 1 day (5 – 4 = 1) and is assigned to the LST segment of activity A. The LFT for activity A is 5 days (1 + 4 = 5) and is assigned to the LFT segment of activity A.

- Because, activities A and B have no preceding activities and are the only activities to start at the beginning of the network, the earliest LST out of either activity A or activity B represents the LST of the network. The LST for the start of the network is calculated as follows:
  - LST of activity B – duration time of start node = 0 days (0 – 0 = 0).
  - LST of activity A – duration time of start node = 1 day (1 – 0 = 1).
  The LST for the start node of the network is 0 days and is assigned to the start node.

- Because, the EST, EFT and LST of the start of the network is 0 days, the LFT of the start node of the network is also 0 days. This is because the start and finish of the start of the network is instantaneous. The LFT is assigned to the start node of the network.

Figure 75 shows network C with the backward pass completed.

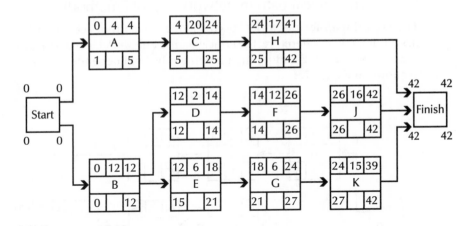

Figure 75 Network C with the backward pass completed

9.2.4 The total, free and independent float possessed by the activities of network C

A summary table of network C, which includes total, free and independent float times, is shown as Table 22. It should be noted that when calculating the float of an activity the relevant times are used.

Table 22 A summary table of network C

Activity	Duration (days)	Start		Finish		Total Float	Free Float	Ind. Float
		EST	LST	EFT	LFT			
A	4	0	1	4	5	1	0	0
B	12	0	0	12	12	0	0	0
C	20	4	5	24	25	1	0	-1
D	2	12	12	14	14	0	0	0
E	6	12	15	18	21	3	0	0
F	12	14	14	26	26	0	0	0
G	6	18	21	24	27	3	0	-3
H	17	24	25	41	42	1	1	0
J	16	26	26	42	42	0	0	0
K	15	24	27	39	42	3	3	0

9.2.5 The critical path in network C (AoN method)

The critical path for network C occurs along the path of activities which has minimal float. Therefore, the critical path for network C occurs through activity nodes B, D, F and J, which is defined by bold dependency arrows, as shown in Figure 76.

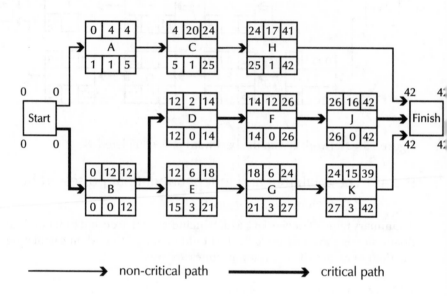

Figure 76 Network C with the critical path defined

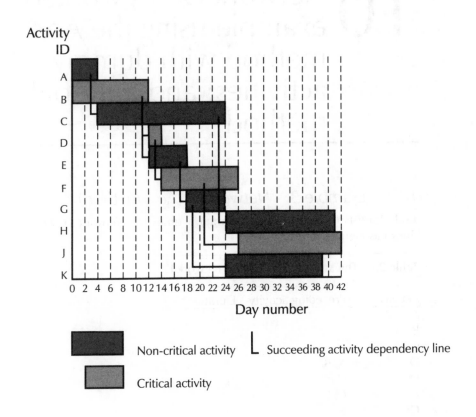

Figure 77   The Gantt chart for network C

10 Network D – A worked example using the AoA method with dummy activities; and the AoN method

10.1 Example 3 – Network D (AoA method)

Table 23 lists the activities and duration times for Network D, which is shown as Figure 78.

Table 23 The table of activities for network D

Activity	Preceding activity	Duration*
A	–	11
B	–	9
C	A	29
D	A, B	26
E	C	16
F	C, D	17
G	E	6
H	F	6

* Duration time in days.

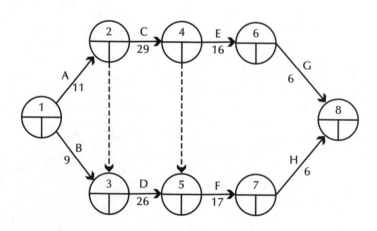

Figure 78 Network D

10.1.1 The drawing of network D (AoA method)

- There are no preceding activities before activities A and B. Activities A and B represent the start of the network and are shown starting from event 1.
- Activity C is dependent upon the prior completion of preceding activity A. Once activity A has finished at event 2, activity C can start from event 2.
- Activity D is dependent upon the prior completion of preceding activities A and B. The dependency of activity D, on the prior completion of activity A, is shown by the dummy activity leading from event 2 to event 3. Once activities A and B have finished, activity D can start from event 3.
- Activity E is dependent upon the prior completion of preceding activity C. Once activity C has finished, activity E can start from event 4.
- Activity F is dependent upon the prior completion of preceding activities C and D. The dependency of succeeding activity F on preceding activity C is shown by the dummy activity leading from event 4 to event 5. Once activities C and D have finished, activity F can start from event 5.
- Activity G is dependent upon the prior completion of preceding activity E. Once activity E has finished at event 6, activity G can start from event 6.
- Activity H is dependent upon the prior completion of activity F. Once activity F has finished at event 7, activity H can start from event 7.
- Activities G and H have no succeeding activities. The completion of activities G and H at event 8 represents the finish of the network.

Network D has 8 activities, 2 dummy activities and 8 events

10.1.2 The forward pass for network D (AoA method)

Calculations involved in the forward pass make use of the following formula:

EST of activity 'X' = EST of preceding activity + its duration time

---

- Event 1 has an EET of 0 days which is assigned to the event. Activities A and B start at day 0.
- Event 2 has an EET of 11 days (0 + 11 = 11) which is assigned to the event. Activity C can start at day 11.
- The EET of event 3 is determined by the latest EFT of the activities which lead into this event. The calculation for event 3 is as follows:

- EFT of activity A and the dummy activity = 11 days (11 + 0 = 11).
- EFT of activity B = 9 days (0 + 9 = 9).

Event 3 has an EET of 11 days which is assigned to the event. Activity D can start at day 11.

- Event 4 has an EET of 40 days (11 + 29 = 40) which is assigned to the event. Activity E can start at day 40.
- The EET of event 5 is determined by the latest EFT of the activities which lead into this event. The calculation for event 5 is as follows:
  - EFT of activity C and the dummy activity = 40 days (40 + 0 = 40).
  - EFT of activity D = 37 days (11 + 26 = 37).

Event 5 has an EET of 40 days which is assigned to the event. Activity F can start at day 40.

- Event 6 has an EET of 56 days (40 + 16 = 56) which is assigned to the event. Activity G can start at day 56.
- Event 7 has an EET of 57 days (40 + 17 = 57) which is assigned to the event. Activity H can start at day 57.
- Event 8 has two activities finishing at it. The EET of event 8 is determined by the latest EFT of the activities which lead into this event. The calculation for event 8 is as follows:
  - EFT of activity G = 62 days (56 + 6 = 62).
  - EFT of activity H = 63 days (57 + 6 = 63).

The EET for event 8 is 63 days which is assigned to the event. Event 8 represents the finish event of Network D.

> **The minimum amount of time required to complete the project is 63 days. Therefore, the TPT for network D is 63 days.**

The completed forward pass for network D is shown as Figure 79.

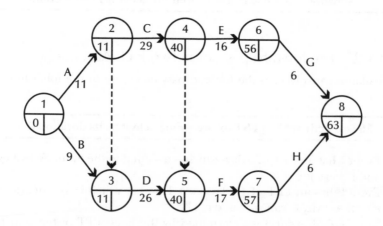

Figure 79 Network D with the forward pass completed

The EET calculations for network D, Figure 79, are shown in tabulated form in Table 24.

Table 24   The EET calculations for network D

Event	Calculations	EET (days)
1	0 + 0 =	0
2	0 + 11 =	11
3	11 + 0 =	11
4	11 + 29 =	40
5	40 + 0 =	40
6	40 + 16 =	56
7	40 + 17 =	57
8	57 + 6 =	63

The backward pass for network D is as follows:

10.1.3   The backward pass for network D (AoA method)

Calculations involved in the backward pass make use of the following formula:

> **LST of activity 'X' = LFT of activity ' X' – its duration time**

- If the TPT of 63 days is to be observed the LET for event 8 will be 63 days.
- Event 7 has an LET of 57 days (63 – 6 = 57) which is assigned to the event. Activity F must finish by day 57 if activity H is to start by its LST.
- Event 6 has an LET of 57 days (63 – 6 = 57) which is assigned to the event. Activity E must finish by day 57 if activity G is to start by its LST.
- Event 5 has an LET of 40 days (57 – 17 = 40) which is assigned to the event. Activities C and D must finish by day 40 if activity F is to start by its LST. Activity C must finish by day 40 because activity F is dependent upon the prior completion of activity C (as shown by the dummy activity leading from event 4 to event 5).
- The LET of event 4 is determined by the earliest LST of the activities which lead from event 4. The calculation for the LET of event 4 is as follows:
  - LST of activity F less the dummy activity = 40 days (40 – 0 = 40).
  - LST of activity E = 41 days (57 – 16 = 41).
  The LET for event 4 is 40 days which is assigned to the event. Activity C must finish by day 40 if activity F is to start by its LST.
- Event 3 has an LET of 14 days (40 – 26 = 14) which is assigned to the event. Activity B must finish by day 14 if activity D is to start by its LST.

- The LET of event 2 is determined by the earliest LST of the activities which start from event 2. The calculation for the LET of event 2 is as follows:
  - LST of activity D less the dummy activity = 14 days (14 – 0 = 14).
  - LST of activity C = 11 days (40 – 29 = 11).

  The LET for event 2 is 11 days which is assigned to the event. Activity A must finish by day 11 if activity C is to start by its LST.
- The LET of event 1 is determined by the earliest LST of the activities which start from event 1. The calculation for the LET of event 1 is as follows:
  - LST of activity B = 5 days (14 – 9 = 5).
  - LST of activity A = 0 days (11 – 11 = 0).

  The LET for event 1 is 0 days which is assigned to the event.

The completed backward pass for network D is shown as Figure 80.

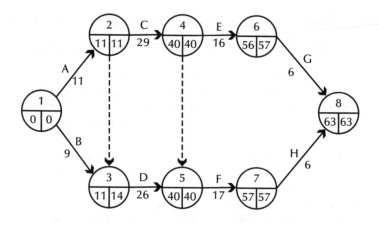

Figure 80   Network D with the backward pass completed

The LET calculations for network D in Figure 80 are shown in tabulated form in Table 25.

Table 25 The LET calculations for network D

Event	Calculations	LET (days)
7	63 – 6 =	57
6	63 – 6 =	57
5	57 – 17 =	40
4	40 – 0 =	40
3	40 – 26 =	14
2	40 – 29 =	11
1	11 – 11 =	0

10.1.4 The total, free and independent float possessed by the activities of network D

A summary table of network D, which includes total, free and independent float times, is shown as Table 26. It should be noted that when calculating the float of an activity the relevant event times are used.

Table 26 A summary table of network D

Activity	Duration (days)	Start		Finish		Total Float	Free Float	Ind Float
		EST	LST	EFT	LFT			
A	11	0	0	11	11	0	0	0
B	9	0	5	9	14	5	2	2
C	29	11	11	40	40	0	0	0
D	26	11	14	37	40	3	3	0
E	16	40	41	56	57	1	0	0
F	17	40	40	57	57	0	0	0
G	6	56	57	62	63	1	1	0
H	6	57	57	63	63	0	0	0

10.1.5 The critical path in network D (AoA method)

The critical path for network D occurs along the path of activities which has minimal float. Therefore, the critical path for network D occurs through activities A, C, F and H (i.e. events 1, 2, 4, 5, 7 and 8). Network D is shown completed as Figure 81.

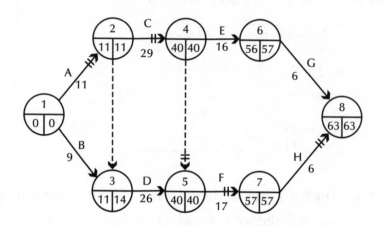

Figure 81 Network D with the critical path defined

10.2 Example 3 – Network D (AoN method)

Table 27 lists the activities and duration times for Network D, which is shown as Figure 82.

Table 27 The table of activities for network D

Activity	Preceding activity	Duration*
A	–	11
B	–	9
C	A	29
D	A, B	26
E	C	16
F	C, D	17
G	E	6
H	F	6

* Duration time in days.

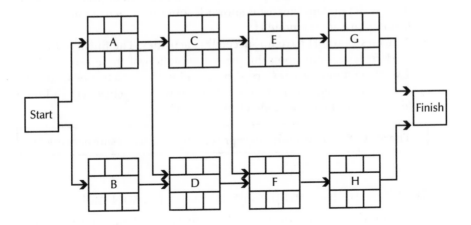

Figure 82 Network D

10.2.1 The drawing of network D (AoN method)

- There are no preceding activities before activities A and B. Two dependency arrows are shown leading from the start node of the network. One dependency arrow leads into an activity node which represents activity A; the other arrow leads into an activity node which represents activity B.
- Two activities are dependent upon the prior completion of activity A (i.e. activities C and D). Therefore, two activity nodes are shown to the right of activity A. One of these activity nodes represents activity C; the other node represents activity D. Two dependency arrows are shown leading from activity A, of which one arrow leads into activity node C while the other arrow leads into activity node D.
- Activity D is also dependent upon the prior completion of activity B (i.e. activity D is dependent upon the prior completion of activities A and B). A dependency arrow is shown leading from activity node B and leading into activity node D.
- Activity E is dependent upon the prior completion of preceding activity C. Once activity C has finished, activity E can start. A dependency arrow is shown leading from activity node C and leading into activity node E.
- Activity F is dependent upon the prior completion of preceding activities C and D. Two dependency arrows are shown leading into activity node F; one arrow is leading into activity F from activity C; the other arrow is leading into activity F from activity D.
- Activity G is dependent upon the prior completion of preceding activity E. A dependency arrow is shown leading from activity node E and leading into activity node G.

105

- Activity H is dependent upon the prior completion of preceding activity F. A dependency arrow is shown leading from activity node F and leading into activity node H.
- Activities G and H have no succeeding activities. The finish of the network is dependent upon the prior completion of these two activities. Two dependency arrows are shown leading from activities G and H, (one arrow from activity G; the other arrow from activity H) and then leading into the finish node of the network.

There are 8 activity nodes to represent the 8 activities of network D

10.2.2   The forward pass for network D (AoN method)

Calculations involved in the forward pass make use of the following formulae:

EST of activity 'X' = EST of preceding activity + its duration time

---

EFT of activity 'X' = EST of activity 'X' + its duration time

---

- Unless clearly stated otherwise, the EST of the start node of the network will be 0 days. Because the start and finish of the start of the network is instantaneous the EFT will also be 0 days. The EST and the EFT are assigned to the start node.
- The EST of activity A is 0 days. This is because activity A starts at the start of the network. The EST of 0 days is assigned to the EST segment of activity A. The EFT for activity A is 11 days (0 + 11 = 11) and is assigned to the EFT segment of activity A.
- The EST of activity B is 0 days. This is because activity B starts at the start of the network. The EST of 0 days is assigned to the EST segment of activity B. The EFT for activity B is 9 days (0 + 9 = 9) and is assigned to the EFT segment of activity B.
- Activity C has only one dependency arrow leading into it (i.e. the arrow from activity A). The EST of activity C is 11 days (0 + 11 = 11) and is assigned to the EST segment of activity C. The EFT for activity C is 40 days (11 + 29 = 40) and is assigned to the EFT segment of activity C.
- Activity D has two dependency arrows leading into it (i.e. the arrow from activity A and the arrow from activity B). The EST of activity D is determined by the preceding activity with the latest completion time. The EST for activity D is calculated as follows:
  - EST of activity A + its duration time = 11 days (0 + 11 = 11).
  - EST of activity B + its duration time = 9 days (0 + 9 = 9).

The EST of activity D is 11 days and is assigned to the EST segment of activity D. The EFT for activity D is 37 days (11 + 26 = 37) and is assigned to the EFT segment of activity D.

- Activity E has only one dependency arrow leading into it (i.e. the arrow from activity C). The EST of activity E is 40 days (11 + 29 = 40) and is assigned to the EST segment of activity E. The EFT for activity E is 56 days (40 + 16 = 56) and is assigned to the EFT segment of activity E.
- Activity F has two dependency arrows leading into it (i.e. the arrow from activity C and the arrow from activity D). The EST of activity F is determined by the preceding activity with the latest completion time. The EST for activity F is calculated as follows:
  - EST of activity C + its duration time = 40 days (11 + 29 = 40).
  - EST of activity D + its duration time = 37 days (11 + 26 = 37).

  The EST of activity F is 40 days and is assigned to the EST segment of activity F. The EFT for activity F is 57 days (40 + 17 = 57) and is assigned to the EFT segment of activity F.
- Activity G has only one dependency arrow leading into it (i.e. the arrow from activity E). The EST of activity G is 56 days (40 + 16 = 56) and is assigned to the EST segment of activity G. The EFT for activity G is 62 days (56 + 6 = 62) and is assigned to the EFT segment of activity G.
- Activity H has only one dependency arrow leading into it (i.e. the arrow from activity F). The EST of activity H is 57 days (40 + 17 = 57) and is assigned to the EST segment of activity H. The EFT for activity H is 63 days (57 + 6 = 63) and is assigned to the EFT segment of activity H.
- The finish node of the network has two dependency arrows leading into it (i.e. the arrows from activities G and H). The EST of the finish node (i.e. the earliest time in which the network can be completed) is determined by the preceding activity with the latest completion time. The EST for the finish node of the network is calculated as follows:
  - EST of activity G + its duration time = 62 days (56 + 6 = 62).
  - EST of activity H + its duration time = 63 days (57 + 6 = 63).

  The EST of the finish node of the network is 63 days and is assigned to the finish node. The EFT, LST and LFT of the finish node will be the same as the EST because the start and finish of the finish of the network is instantaneous.

The minimum amount of time required to complete the project is 63 days. Therefore, the TPT for network D is 63 days.

Network D is shown with the forward pass completed as Figure 83.

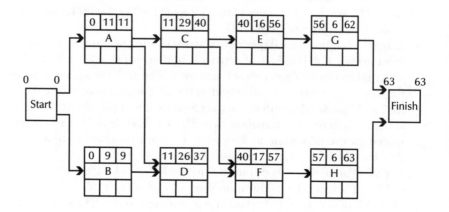

Figure 83   Network D with the forward pass completed

10.2.3   The backward pass for network D (AoN method)

Calculations involved in the backward pass make use of the following formulae:

> **LST of activity 'X' = LST of succeeding activity – duration time of activity 'X'**

> **LFT of activity 'X' = LST of activity 'X' + its duration time**

- The LST for activity H is determined by subtracting the duration time of activity H from the LST of the finish node. The LST for activity H is 57 days (63 – 6 = 57) and is assigned to the LST segment of activity H. The LFT for activity H is 63 days (57 + 6 = 63) and is assigned to the LFT segment of activity H.
- The LST for activity G is determined by subtracting the duration time of activity G from the LST of the finish node. The LST for Activity G is 57 days (63 – 6 = 57) and is assigned to the LST segment of activity G. The LFT for activity G is 63 days (57 + 6 = 63) and is assigned to the LFT segment of activity G.
- The LST for activity F is determined by subtracting the duration time of activity F from the LST of activity H. The LST for activity F is 40 days (57 – 17 = 40) and is assigned to the LST segment of activity F. The LFT for activity F is 57 days (40 + 17 = 57) and is assigned to the LFT segment of activity F.

- The LST for activity E is determined by subtracting the duration time of activity E from the LST of activity G. The LST for activity E is 41 days ($57 - 16 = 41$) and is assigned to the LST segment of activity E. The LFT for activity E is 57 days ($41 + 16 = 57$) and is assigned to the LFT segment of activity E.
- The LST for activity D is determined by subtracting the duration time of activity D from the LST of activity F. The LST for activity D is 14 days ($40 - 26 = 14$) and is assigned to the LST segment of activity D. The LFT for activity D is 40 days ($14 + 26 = 40$) and is assigned to the LFT segment of activity D.
- The LST for activity C is determined by the smallest value obtained from subtracting the duration time of activity C from the LST of each activity which succeeds activity C (i.e. activities E and F). The LST for activity C is calculated as follows:
  - LST of activity F – duration time of activity C = 11 days ($40 - 29 = 11$).
  - LST of activity E – duration time of activity C = 12 days ($41 - 29 = 12$).
  The LST of activity C is 11 days and is assigned to the LST segment of activity C. The LFT for activity C is 40 days ($11 + 29 = 40$) and is assigned to the LFT segment of activity C.
- The LST for activity B is determined by subtracting the duration time of activity B from the LST of activity D. The LST for activity B is 5 days ($14 - 9 = 5$) and is assigned to the LST segment of activity B. The LFT for activity B is 14 days ($5 + 9 = 14$) and is assigned to the LFT segment of activity B.
- The LST for activity A is determined by the smallest value obtained from subtracting the duration time of activity A from the LST of each activity which succeeds activity A (i.e. activities C and D). The LST for activity A is calculated as follows:
  - LST of activity D – duration time of activity A = 3 days ($14 - 11 = 3$).
  - LST of activity C – duration time of activity A = 0 days ($11 - 11 = 0$).
  The LST of activity A is 0 days and is assigned to the LST segment of activity A. The LFT for activity A is 11 days ($0 + 11 = 11$) and is assigned to the LFT segment of activity A.
- Because activities A and B have no preceding activities, and are also the only activities to start at the beginning of the network, the earliest LST out of either activity A or activity B represents the LST of the network. The LST for the start of the network is calculated as follows:
  - LST of activity B – duration time of start node = 5 days ($5 - 0 = 5$).
  - LST of activity A – duration time of start node = 0 days ($0 - 0 = 0$).
  The LST for the start node of the network is 0 days and is assigned to the start node.
- Because the EST, EFT and LST of the start of the network is 0 days, the LFT of the network is also 0 days. This is because the start and finish of the start of the network is instantaneous. The LFT is assigned to the start node of the network.

Figure 84 shows network D with the backward pass completed.

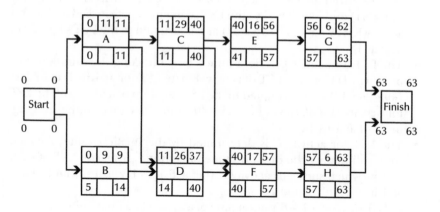

Figure 84 Network D with the backward pass completed

10.2.4 The total, free and independent float possessed by the activities of network D

A summary table of network D, which includes total, free and independent float times, is shown as Table 28. It should be noted that when calculating the float of an activity the relevant times are used.

Table 28 A summary table of network D

Activity	Duration (days)	Start		Finish		Total Float	Free Float	Ind. Float
		EST	LST	EFT	LFT			
A	11	0	0	11	11	0	0	0
B	9	0	5	9	14	5	2	2
C	29	11	11	40	40	0	0	0
D	26	11	14	37	40	3	3	0
E	16	40	41	56	57	1	0	0
F	17	40	40	57	57	0	0	0
G	6	56	57	62	63	1	1	0
H	6	57	57	63	63	0	0	0

10.2.5 The critical path in network D (AoN method)

The critical path for network D occurs along the path of activities which has minimal float. Therefore, the critical path for network D occurs through activity nodes A, C, F and H, which is defined by bold dependency arrows, as shown in Figure 85.

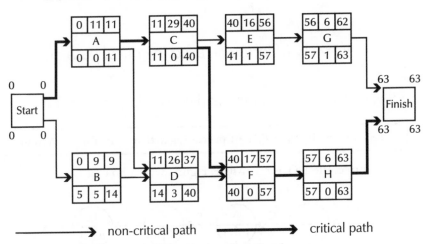

Figure 85 Network D with the critical path defined

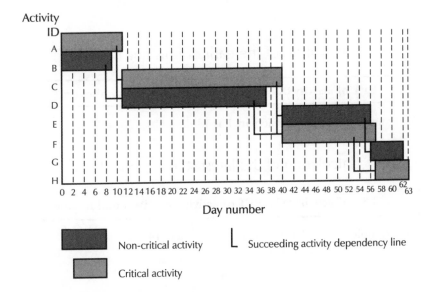

Figure 86 The Gantt chart for network D

11 Formulae used in critical path analysis and the AoN method

11.1 A review of formulae used in critical path analysis

11.1.1 Calculation of the earliest starting time (EST)

> **EST of activity 'X' = EST of preceding activity + its duration time**

For example, the EST for activity F, Figure 87, is 10 days $(3 + 7 = 10)$.

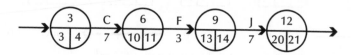

Figure 87   Activity F

11.1.2 Calculation of the earliest finishing time (EFT)

> **EFT of activity 'X' = EST of activity 'X' + its duration time**

For example, the EFT for activity F is 13 days $(10 + 3 = 13)$.

11.1.3 Calculation of the latest starting time (LST)

> **LST of activity 'X' = LFT of activity 'X' – its duration time**

For example, the LST for activity F is 11 days $(14 – 3 = 11)$.

11.1.4   Calculation of the latest finishing time (LFT)

> **LFT of activity 'X' = LFT of succeeding activity – its duration time**

For example, the LFT for activity F is 14 days (21 – 7 = 14).

11.1.5   The earliest event time (EET)

> **EET of event 'X' = EET of preceding event + duration time of the activity**

For example, the EET for event 6 is 10 days (3 + 7 = 10).

11.1.6   The latest event time (LET)

> **LET of event 'X' = LET of succeeding event – duration time of the activity**

For example, the LET for event 6 is 11 days (14 – 3 = 11).

11.2   A review of formulae used in the AoN method

11.2.1   Calculation of the earliest starting time (EST)

> **EST of activity 'X' = EST of preceding activity + its duration time**

For example, the EST for activity F, Figure 88, is 10 days (3 + 7 = 10).

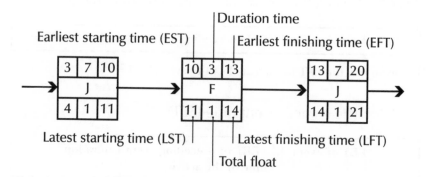

Figure 88 Activity F

11.2.2 Calculation of the earliest finishing time (EFT)

EFT of activity 'X' = EST of activity 'X' + its duration time

For example, the EFT for activity F is 13 days (10 + 3 = 13).

11.2.3 Calculation of the latest starting time (LST)

LST of activity 'X' = LST of succeeding activity – duration time of activity 'X'

For example, the LST for activity F is 11 days (14 – 3 = 11).

11.2.4 Calculation of the latest finishing time (LFT)

LFT of activity 'X' = LST of activity 'X' + its duration time

For example, the LFT for activity F is 14 days (11 + 3 = 14).

11.3 A review of formulae used in critical path analysis to calculate float

11.3.1 Total float

> **(LET of succeeding event – EET of preceding event) – duration time of activity**

For example, the total float possessed by activity F is 1 day; i.e. $(14 - 10) - 3 = 1$.

11.3.2 Free float

> **(EET of succeeding event – EET of preceding event) – duration time of activity**

For example, the free float possessed by activity F is 0 days; i.e. $(13 - 10) - 3 = 0$

11.3.3 Independent float

> **Minimum time available to complete activity – duration time**

NB: Minimum time available = EET of succeeding event – LET of preceding event.

The independent float possessed by activity F is -1 day; i.e. $(13 - 11) - 3 = -1$.

11.4   A review of formulae used in the AoN method to calculate float

11.4.1   Total float

Total float of activity 'X' = LST activity 'X' – EST of activity 'X'

The total float possessed by activity F is 1 day $(11 - 10 = 1)$.

11.4.2   Free float

Free float of = the LFT of activity 'X' which will not affect – EFT of **activity 'X'   the float in a succeeding activity   activity 'X'**

The total float possessed by activity F is 1 day $(13 - 13 = 0)$.

11.4.3   Independent float

Ind. float = the LFT of activity 'X' – the EST of activity – duration **of activity   which will not affect   'X' which will not   time of** **'X'   the float of a   affect the float of   activity 'X'** **   succeeding activity   a preceding activity**

The independent float possessed by activity F is 1 day; i.e. $(13 - 11) - 3 = -1$.

12 Questions on critical path analysis and the AoN method

Requirement

Draw the network (as an AoA network, and as an AoN network) for each of the following tables of activities and:

- Complete the forward pass and calculate the TPT.
- Complete the backward pass for both networks and calculate the total float for each activity in the AoN network.
- Identify the critical path.
- Complete a summary table (which is to include total float and free float).
- Draw the Gantt chart.

12.1 Question 1 – Network E

Table of activities for network E

Activity	Preceding activity	Duration*
A	–	5
B	A	8
C	B	7
D	B	4
E	B	2
F	C	6
G	D	12
H	E	9
J	F	4
K	H	2

* Duration time in days.

12.2   Question 2 – Network F

Table of activities for network F

Activity	Preceding activity	Duration*
A	–	5
B	–	8
C	–	4
D	–	3
E	A	15
F	B	11
G	C	17
H	D	12
J	E, F	5
K	G, H	6

* Duration time in days.

12.3   Question 3 – Network G

Table of activities for network G

Activity	Precedes activity	Duration (Days)
A	D, E	21
B	F	37
C	G, H	29
D	J	5
E	K	48
F	K	27
G	K	41
H	L	4
J	–	44
K	–	4
L	–	40

12.4   Question 4 – Network H

Table of activities for network H

Activity	Preceding activity	Duration
A	–	25 d
B	–	58 d
C	A	28 d
D	A	32 d
E	A	46 d
F	C	6 d
G	C	15 d
H	C	16 d
J	B, D, F	11 d
K	G, J	2 d
L	G, J	1 d
M	E, H, K	2 d
N	E, H, K, L	4 d

12.5   Question 5 – Network J

Table of activities for network J

Activity	Precedes activity	Duration*
A	D, E, F, J	8
B	E, J	10
C	F	9
D	G, H	12
E	H	8
F	K	14
G	K	6
H	K	7
J	–	17
K	–	2

* Duration time in weeks.

12.6 Question 6 – 12

6 Write a management summary that gives an overview on critical path analysis and the AoN method.

7 Discuss the possible benefits of CPA and the AoN method, if used by a small manufacturing company which is planning to move premises (including all fixed assets) from one part of the country to another.

8 Discuss what advantages critical path analysis and the AoN method would have to the projects manager of a company which has sub-contracted some of the activities of a project to various sub-contractors.

9 What cultural problems could occur within an organisation which has imposed critical path analysis and the AoN method?

10 Why is it particularly important to maintain an attention of a non-critical path which is near to the TPT?

11 Suggest various applications for the use of computer software AoA and AoN programs within the internal environment of business.

12 Produce a table of activities and draw the derived network for a one-day training session for the sales force of a company, which is to be held at an external venue.

13 Answers to questions 1 – 5 of Chapter 12

13.1   Answers to question 1 – Network E

The AoA network diagram for network E

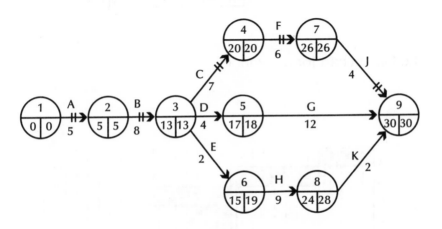

The summary table for the activities of network E

Activity	Duration (days)	Start Earliest	Start Latest	Finish Earliest	Finish Latest	Total Float	Free Float
A	5	0	0	5	5	0	0
B	8	5	5	13	13	0	0
C	7	13	13	20	20	0	0
D	4	13	14	17	18	1	0
E	2	13	17	15	19	4	0
F	6	20	20	26	26	0	0
G	12	17	18	29	30	1	1
H	9	15	19	24	28	4	0
J	4	26	26	30	30	0	0
K	2	24	28	26	30	4	4

The AoN network diagram for network E

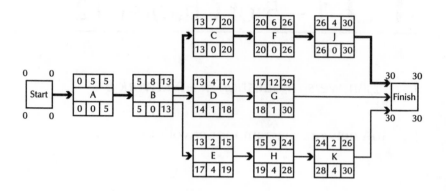

The Gantt chart for network E

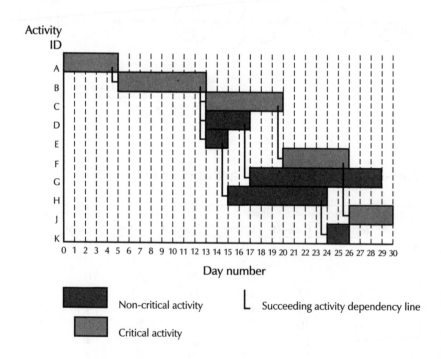

13.2   Answers to question 2 – Network F

The AoA network diagram for network F

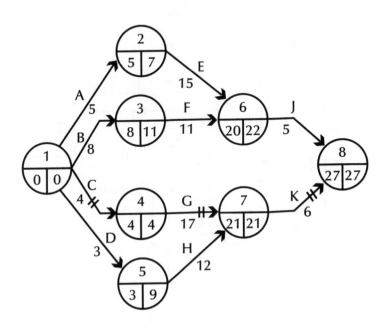

The summary table for the activities of network F

Activity	Duration (days)	Start		Finish		Total Float	Free Float
		Earliest	Latest	Earliest	Latest		
A	5	0	2	5	7	2	0
B	8	0	3	8	11	3	0
C	4	0	0	4	4	0	0
D	3	0	6	3	9	6	0
E	15	5	7	20	22	2	0
F	11	8	11	19	22	3	1
G	17	4	4	21	21	0	0
H	12	3	9	15	21	6	6
J	5	20	22	25	27	2	2
K	6	21	21	27	27	0	0

The AoN network diagram for network F

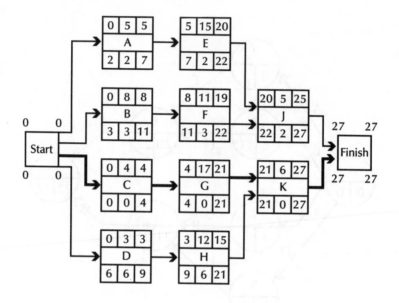

The Gantt chart for network F

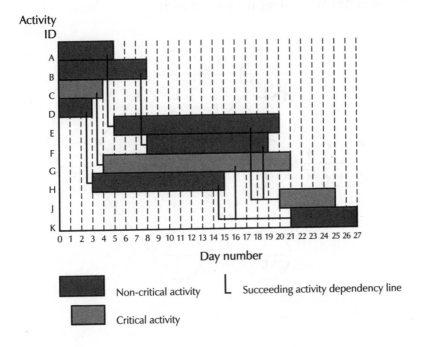

Activity
ID

Day number

Non-critical activity   L Succeeding activity dependency line

Critical activity

13.3 Answers to question 3 – Network G

The AoA network diagram for network G

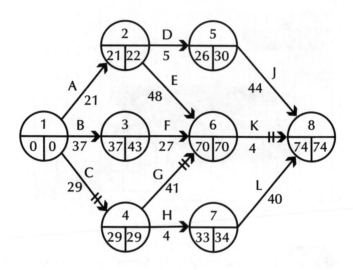

The summary table for the activities of network G

Activity	Duration (days)	Start Earliest	Start Latest	Finish Earliest	Finish Latest	Total Float	Free Float
A	21	0	1	21	22	1	0
B	37	0	6	37	43	6	0
C	29	0	0	29	29	0	0
D	5	21	25	26	30	4	0
E	48	21	22	69	70	1	1
F	27	37	43	64	70	6	6
G	41	29	29	70	70	0	0
H	4	29	30	33	34	1	0
J	44	26	30	70	74	4	4
K	4	70	70	74	74	0	0
L	40	33	34	73	74	1	1

The AoN network diagram for Network G

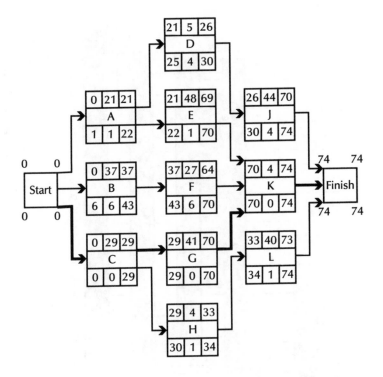

The Gantt chart for network G

Activity ID

Day number

Non-critical activity

Critical activity

⌐ Succeeding activity dependency line

13.4   Answers to question 4 – Network H

The AoA network diagram for network H

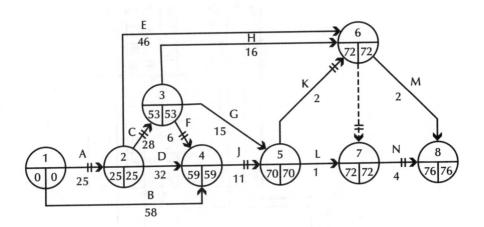

The summary table for the activities of network H

Activity	Duration (days)	Start		Finish		Total Float	Free Float
		Earliest	Latest	Earliest	Latest		
A	25	0	0	25	25	0	0
B	58	0	1	58	59	1	1
C	28	25	25	53	53	0	0
D	32	25	27	57	59	2	2
E	46	25	26	71	72	1	1
F	6	53	53	59	59	0	0
G	15	53	55	68	70	2	2
H	16	53	56	69	72	3	3
J	11	59	59	70	70	0	0
K	2	70	70	72	72	0	0
L	1	70	71	71	72	1	1
M	2	72	74	74	76	2	2
N	4	72	72	76	76	0	0

The AoN network diagram for network H

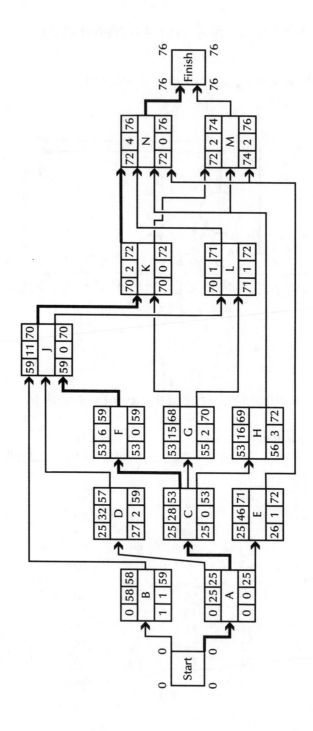

The Gantt chart for network H

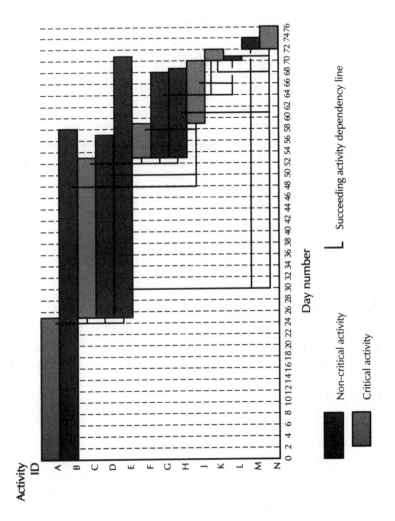

13.5 Answers to question 5 – Network J

The AoA network diagram for network J

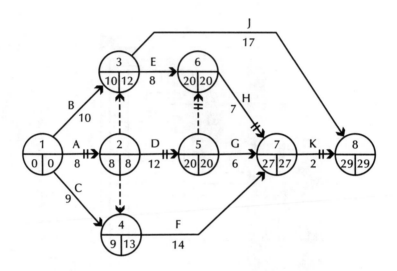

The summary table for the activities of network J

Activity	Duration (weeks)	Start Earliest	Latest	Finish Earliest	Latest	Total Float	Free Float
A	8	0	0	8	8	0	0
B	10	0	2	10	12	2	0
C	9	0	4	9	13	4	0
D	12	8	8	20	20	0	0
E	8	10	12	18	20	2	2
F	14	9	13	23	27	4	4
G	6	20	21	26	27	1	1
H	7	20	20	27	27	0	0
J	17	10	12	27	29	2	2
K	2	27	27	29	29	0	0

The AoN network diagram for network J

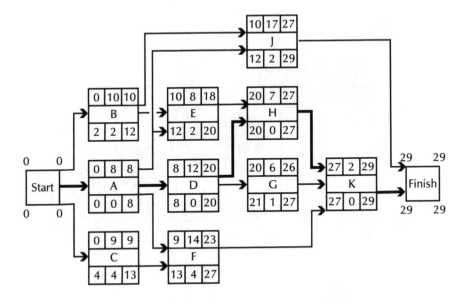

The Gantt chart for network J

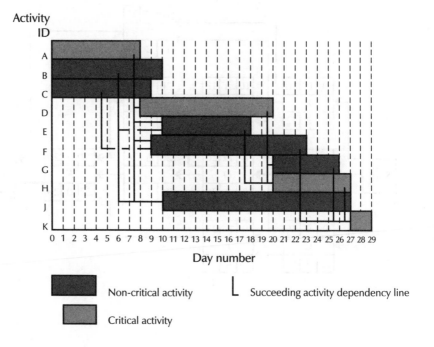

Chapter 14   Glossary

Activity. A task (e.g. *Fit doors*) which is performed as a part of the overall project. The term activity involves the passage of time (e.g. *Wait for glue to set*) and does not necessarily mean that actual 'physical' work (e.g. *Fit doors*) is carried out.

Activity on Arrow (AoA) network. The pictorial representation of the activities of a project, and the relationships between these activities, through the use of a network diagram which consists of arrows (which represent the activities) and events, often referred to as nodes, (which represent points in time during the progress of the project). Sometimes referred to as the arrow diagramming method (ADM). Time flows from left to right in an AoA network.

Activity on Node (AoN) network. The pictorial representation of the activities of a project, and the relationships between these activities, through the use of a network diagram which consists of nodes (which represent the activities) and arrows, often referred to as dependency arrows, (which represent the relationships between the activities and the progression of the project). Time flows from left to right in an AoN network.

Activities in series. Activities which take place one after the other along the same path. Unless stated otherwise, an activity in series is dependent upon the prior completion of its predecessor (i.e. the current activity starts after the preceding activity has finished).

Activity arrow. Pictorial symbol used to define an activity in an Activity on Arrow network.

ADM. *See* Arrow diagramming method

Arrow diagramming method (ADM). *See* Activity on Arrow (AoA) network.

As Late As Possible (ALAP). A constraint which is placed upon an activity so that the activity occurs as late as possible without delaying a succeeding activity.

ALAP. *See* As late as possible.

As Soon As Possible (ASAP). A constraint which is placed upon an activity so that the activity occurs as early as possible without affecting the logic of the network. ASAP is the nominal constraint used in critical path analysis.

ASAP. *See* As soon as possible.

Backward pass. The process of calculating the latest event time (LET); the latest finishing time (LFT) and the latest starting time (LST) of the activities which make-up the network. The backward pass progresses from right-to-left across the network (i.e. the process starts at the finish of the network, and finishes at the start of the network).

Base calendar. The calendar for the project or a group of resources (e.g. the sales work force of a company). The base calendar details the nominal working and non-working days, the working hours and non-working hours (e.g. lunch time), holiday periods and custom working and non-working time periods.

Baseline plan. *See* Original plan.

Bottom-up approach. The most subordinate activities are first identified and then collected into groups, each of which is represented as a summary activity. These groups are then organised into larger groups, each of which is represented by a summary activity, until the summary activities denote the major stages of the project.

Burst node. The term given to a node which has one (or more) activities ending at it, and more than one activity starting from it.

Chain of activities. A path of activities which are linked in series. In a chain of activities, a succeeding activity can not start until the preceding activity has finished.

Closing event. The last event within the network, which thus represents the closing of the network and the finish of the project. Sometimes referred to as the closing node.

Closing node. *See* Closing event.

CPA. *See* Critical path analysis.

CPM. Acronym for critical path method. An alternative term for CPA.

Crashing. The process of reducing the overall duration time of the critical path and the TPT. Such a process involves reducing the duration time of the critical activities which occur along the critical path.

Critical activities. Activities which occur along the critical path.

Critical path. The path of activities whose totalled duration time equates to the minimum overall time required to complete the project. This minimum overall time is referred to as the total project time (TPT). The activities which occur along the critical path will nominally possess no float time.

Critical path analysis (CPA). The pictorial representation, by the use of an arrow network, of the activities which make up a project. Through analysis of the construction of the network, the total project time (TPT), the float times and the critical path can be defined.

Current activity. The activity under immediate, present consideration and to which all relevant analysis of any other activities relates. A preceding activity occurs prior to the current activity; a succeeding activity occurs after the current activity.

Dangling activity. An activity which when completed, enters an event which represents neither the start point of another activity nor the finish of the network. A dangling activity can occur due to ambiguity when defining an activity, or an error when drawing the network.

Dependency. The term used to denote the relationship of an activity in regards to another activity. The dependency relationship is pictorially defined by the dependent activity starting from the head event of the activity on which it depends. This event is the tail event of the activity which is starting.

Dependency arrow. Method used to pictorially define the dependency relationship between activities in an Activity on Node (AoN) network.

Dummy activity. Used in an Activity on Arrow (AoA) network to denote the dependent relationship between an activity and other activities within the network so as to preserve the logic of the network. Dummy activities have no duration time, they do not use-up resources and are pictorially defined as a dotted arrow.

Duration time – planned. The planned time required to complete an activity.

Duration time – actual. The actual amount of time an activity takes to complete in comparison to its planned duration time.

Duration time – planned/actual variance. The difference between the planned duration time, which is assigned to an activity in the original plan, and the actual duration time taken to complete the activity.

Earliest event time (EET). The earliest time by which any event can take place (i.e. start or finish) while still maintaining the total project time (TPT) and the logic of the network.

Earliest finishing time (EFT). The earliest time by which an activity can finish while still maintaining the total project time (TPT) and the logic of the network.

Earliest starting time (EST). The earliest time by which an activity can start while still maintaining the total project time (TPT) and the logic of the network.

EET/LET matrix. A method of calculating and displaying event times and determining which events occur along the critical path.

EFT. *See* Earliest finishing time.

End event of a network. The event which represents the finish of the network. Also referred to as the finish event of the network.

EST. *See* Earliest Starting Time.

Event. A defined point within the project, which absorbs neither time nor resources. An event occurs at the exact point after the finish of a preceding activity and before the start of a succeeding activity.

Finish event of a network. The event which represents the finish or the end of the network The finish event of a network has no succeeding events and therefore no activities start from the finish event.

Finish node. The node which represents the finish or end of the network.

Finish no earlier than (FNET). A constraint which is placed upon an activity so that the activity does not finish before a specified time.

Finish no later than (FNLT). A constraint which is placed upon an activity so that the activity does not finish after a specified time.

Finish to finish (FF). A relationship between two activities whereby an activity finishes at the same time as the preceding activity.

Finish to start (FS). A relationship between two activities whereby the preceding activity must finish before the succeeding activity can start.

Fixed duration scheduling. The duration of an activity remains the same regardless of the level of resources assigned to the activity. Therefore, an increase in the amount of resources used to complete the activity will not reduce the time the activity takes to complete. This method of scheduling is used when it is known that the duration time of the activity will always remain the same.

FNET. *See* Finish no earlier than.

FNLT. *See* Finish no later than.

Following activity. An activity which occurs after the preceding activity. A following activity is normally referred to as a succeeding activity.

Forward pass. The process of calculating the earliest event time (EET); the earliest starting time (EST) and the earliest finishing time (EFT) of the activities which make up a project. The forward pass also calculates the total project time (TPT).

Free float. The amount of float time which can be used-up to complete the activity without affecting the earliest starting time (EST) of a succeeding activity and, therefore, will not alter the amount of float in the succeeding activity.

Fully-allocated. The condition of a resource when it has been assigned a work requirement which is equal to the maximum work achievable capacity of the resource.

Fully-loaded. *See* Fully-allocated.

Gantt bar. The graphical representation of an activity within a Gantt chart. A Gantt bar can define the duration time of an activity and also what type the activity is (e.g. non-critical; milestone). It is possible for a Gantt bar to define a wide variety of information (e.g. the float possessed by the activity).

Gantt chart. Named after its inventor Henry L. Gantt. A graphical representation of a project. The activities of the project are represented by Gantt bars with the relationship between the activities being defined by the relative position of the Gantt bars and the use of succeeding activity dependency lines. A Gantt chart can have an associated table (referred to as the Gantt table) which contains tabulated information about the activities of the project (e.g. activity name; duration time; scheduled start; scheduled finish).

Gantt table. A table which contains information about the activities within a project (e.g. activity name; duration time; resource(s) used; scheduled start; scheduled finish; float). The Gantt table tabulates information pictorially displayed in the Gantt chart.

Hard project. A project where there are few unknowns which results in being able to plan the project to a high degree of accuracy. A hard project is the opposite of a soft project.

Head event. Term used to describe the event at which an activity arrow enters and finishes.

Independent float. The amount of float time possessed by an activity which can be used without affecting the amount of float possessed by either a preceding or succeeding activity.

Lag time. A specific amount of time which is used as a delay between two activities

Latest event time (LET). The latest time by which an event can take place (i.e. start or finish) while still maintaining the total project time (TPT) and the logic of the network.

Latest finishing time (LFT). The latest time by which an activity can finish while still maintaining the total project time (TPT) and the logic of the network.

Latest starting time (LST). The latest time by which an activity can start while still maintaining the total project time (TPT) and the logic of the network.

Lead time. A specific amount of time by which an activity can start before the finish of another activity.

LET. *See* Latest event time.

LFT. *See* Latest finishing time.

Listing activities. The process of presenting in tabulated form, the activities and information relating to those activities which make up the project.

Loading. The assigning to a resource of the work requirement of an activity.

Looping. Term used to define a type of error which can be made while drawing the network. The error results in a group of activities being dependent upon each other on a constantly re-occurring basis so that a preceding activity becomes dependent upon a succeeding activity and a preceding event becomes dependent upon a succeeding event.

LST. *See* Latest starting time.

Master project. A project within which one or more activities represent a sub-project.

Matrix. *See* EET/LET Matrix.

Maximum work achievable capacity (MWAC). The largest amount of work requirement that can be undertaken by a resource before the resource becomes overloaded. The maximum work achievable capacity is sometimes referred to as the resource ceiling.

Merge node. The term given to an event which has more than one activity ending at it (i.e. entering it) and one or more activities subsequently starting from it (i.e. leading from it).

Milestone. An important event or activity within the network which is used as a reference point. An activity which is defined as a milestone will normally have a duration time of zero (this does not mean that the activity is a dummy activity).

Most optimistic duration time. Used in PERT. The estimated minimum amount of time required to complete an activity.

Most pessimistic duration time. Used in PERT. The estimated maximum amount of time required to complete an activity.

Most probable duration time. Used in PERT. The estimated most likely amount of time required to complete an activity.

Multiple activity duration time estimating. *See* PERT.

Must finish on. A constraint which is placed upon an activity so that the activity must finish at a specified time.

Must start on. A constraint which is placed upon an activity so that the activity must start at a specified time.

Negative float time. Can occur when a scheduled time has been assigned to an event. The value of the negative float equates to the required reduction in the duration time of an activity so that the scheduled time can be realized.

Nested sub-projects. Sub-projects which are hierarchically organized within other sub-projects which in turn are hierarchically organized within the master project.

Network. The pictorial representation of the activities which make up a project and denotes the sequence of occurrence and relationship between these activities and the time periods associated with the project.

Node. A node can be a circle which pictorially represent an event in an Activity on Arrow (AoA) network, or a square which pictorially represents an activity in an Activity on Node (AoN) network. A node is often referred to as an event.

Non-critical path. A path of activities in a network which possess float.

Opening event of a network. The start point of the network. There are no preceding events before the opening event and no activities enter the opening event.

Opening node of a network. *See* Opening event of a network.

Outlining. The process of organising the activities of a project in a hierarchical order. Outlining can be carried out by the top-down process, or the bottom-up process.

Original plan. Title given to the plan of the project after it has been compiled at the planning stage. A copy is made of the original plan and this copy is subsequently used during the life-cycle of the project to compare planned progress against actual progress of a project. The original plan is sometimes referred to as the baseline.

Parallel activities. Groups of activities which can occur at the same time but along different paths within the network.

Path. A chain of activities which are linked together.

PERT. Acronym for Program Evaluation and Review Technique. PERT involves the use of three estimated duration times for each activity (i.e. most optimistic, most probable and most pessimistic). Often applied to soft projects where there are a great many unknowns.

PERT chart. The graphical representation of the schedule of a project which shows the dependency relationship between the activities in the project. The chart comprises of a series of nodes, each of which represents an activity, and arrows which define the dependency relationships between the activities. Often used in computer software packages which apply the AoN method.

PDM. *See* Precedence Diagramming Method.

Planned duration time. The duration time assigned to an activity in the original plan.

Precedence diagramming method (PDM). A networking technique used to facilitate the four forms of dependency (and the value of lead time or lag time) which can exist between activities. These four forms of dependency are: finish to start (FS); finish to finish (FF); start to start (SS); start to finish (SF).

Precedence network. *See* Precedence diagramming method.

Preceding activity. The activity which occurs prior to a succeeding activity.

Preceding event. An event which occurs before a succeeding event.

Project. The term given to the collective group total of all the activities of a planned undertaking.

Project life-cycle. Term used to collectively describe the phases through which a project passes.

Resource allocation. The allocation of resources to the activities within a project. Resource allocation does not guarantee optimum efficiency in the allocation of resources because the process takes place at the planning stage rather than when the project is underway.

Resource allocation conflict. A situation which can be caused due to the over-allocation of a resource. Resource allocation conflict can be addressed through the process of levelling.

Resource allocation histogram. Pictorial method of representing the allocation of a resource over a period of time. The histogram permits easier identification of the over-allocation and under-allocation of a resource.

Resource aggregation. The calculation of the total resources required for each time span contained within a project. The total resources required for each time span is calculated by analysing each individual time span and progressively adding together, by working across the network, how much each resource is used within each time span.

Resource calendar. The calendar for a particular resource (e.g. the sales manager) which details the nominal working and non-working days, the working hours and non-working hours (e.g. lunch time), holiday periods and custom working and non-working time periods.

Resource ceiling. *See* Maximum work achievable capacity (MWAC).

Resource-driven scheduling. The duration time of an activity is determined by the level of work required and the amount of resource allocated to execute the work. To a considerable extent, the greater the amount of resource allocated the less the duration time.

Resource levelling. The process of reducing the peaks and troughs of resource usage so that the use of the resource becomes more uniform. Resource levelling is also used to address the issue of resource allocation conflict by using the float time possessed by activities. Sometimes referred to as smoothing.

Scheduling. The assigning of a date / time to an activity.

Schedule date. A specified date which is imposed upon the project as a whole or in part.

Sequential activities. *See* Activities in series.

Sequential numbering. Process of numbering events so as to correctly define their logical sequence of occurrence.

Slack. The difference, as a value of time, between the earliest event time (EET) and the latest event time (LET) of an event. Slack at the tail event of an activity is referred to as tail slack and any utilisation of this slack, under most circumstances, will affect preceding and succeeding events. Slack at the head event of an activity is referred to as head slack and any utilisation of this slack, under most circumstances, will affect succeeding events only.

Slipping. The process of manoeuvring the start time of an activity within its float time. Slipping is only possible when activities possess float. The degree to which an activity can be slipped depends upon the type and amount of float which is possessed by the activity.

Smoothing. *See* Resource levelling.

Soft project. A project where there are many unknowns which results in not being able to plan the project to a high degree of accuracy. Opposite of a hard project.

Start event of a network. The event which represents the start of the network The start event of a network has no preceding events and has no activities finishing at this event.

Start node. The node which represents the start of the network. The start node of a network has no preceding nodes.

Sub-activities. A group of related activities which can be collectively represented as a summary activity within a large project. The sub-activities represent the work which is required to be completed in order to complete the summary activity.

Sub-projects. The complexity of a large project can result in the need to divide the project into smaller, and hence more manageable phases. These smaller phases are referred to as sub-projects. This hierarchical organisation of activities within a project can be based on different criteria (e.g. specific summary activities; areas of managerial responsibility; contractual assignment such as sub-contracting).

Succeeding activity. An activity which occurs after a preceding activity.

Succeeding event. An event which occurs after a preceding event.

Succeeding node. An node which occurs after a preceding node.

Summary activity. An activity used to define a major phase in a project. A summary activity will often have one or more subordinate activities which are part of the phase of the project which the summary activity represents.

Symbol – (use of). Used in the table of activities either at the start of the table, so as to denote the activity has no preceding activity (i.e. the start of the network), or at the end of the table so as to denote that there is no succeeding activity (i.e. the finish of the network).

Table of activities. The activities of the project presented in a tabulated format. The information contained in the table nominally consists of the ID of each activity (e.g. a letter, number or generalised description of the activity to be undertaken), the duration time for each activity and the relationships between the activities.

Tail event. Term sometimes used to define the event at the start point of an activity.

Task. *See* Activity.

Top-down approach. A method used when constructing a project. With this method the major phases of a project are identified first and then the activities which are required to be undertaken, so as to meet these major phases, are defined. Then, any activities which are subordinate to the activities which are required to be undertaken so as to complete the major phases, are detailed. The process of identifying each level of subordinate activity is continued until all the activities of a project have been identified. This method of constructing a project is the opposite to the bottom-up approach.

Total float. The maximum amount of spare time which is possessed by an activity. Total float occurs when the earliest starting time (EST) of an activity and the latest starting time (LST) of its succeeding activity are at their maximum distance apart.

Total project time (TPT). The combined total of all the duration times of the activities which occur along the critical path. This total project time denotes the minimum time in which the project can be completed.

Tracking. The process of regularly updating the schedule of a project and comparing the schedule to the original plan of the project. Tracking assists in identifying activities which have been slipped, are delayed or have started (or finished) early.

Under-allocated. When a resource has been assigned a work requirement which is below the maximum work achievable capacity (MWAC) of the resource. Sometimes referred to as under-loaded.

Unit content. The numerical quantity of a resource. A resource which consists of five workmen, each of whom represents one unit, will have a unit content of 5 units.

Unique event number. A numerical identity which is assigned to, and is unique to, each individual event in the network. Each number is unique so as to avoid ambiguity. Event numbers can progressively increase, from one event to the next event, by a factor of 1 or by another factor (e.g. 10). A factor of 10 could be used at the preliminary design stage of a complex project where there is a considerable degree of uncertainty as to how many events should be drawn in the network.

Unique identity. The resultant identity obtained by the provision of a unique letter to each of the activities in a project.

Unique letter. The identity letter which is given to each individual activity in a project where space or other factors deny a more descriptive meaning being attached to each activity.

Under-loaded. *See* Under-allocated.

Updating. *See* Tracking.

Work requirement. The work content of an activity, expressed as a nominal value (e.g. hours), which is required to be carried out in order that the activity be completed.

12 or 24 hour clock. Time format which can be used during the assigning and analysis of the EET, LET, EST, EFT LST and LFT.

Index

Further reading

- Lockyer K. G. and Gordon J. (1991) *Critical Path Analysis and Other Network Techniques,* Fifth Edition. Pitman Publishing, London.

- Lockyer K. (1995) *Project Management and Project Network Techniques,* Sixth Edition. Pitman Publishing, London.

- Lock, Dennis. (1996) *Project Management,* Sixth Edition. Gower Publishing, Aldershot.